G000245125

ROCKY'S plaice

Holiday club programme

for 5- to 11-year-olds

© Dave Godfrey 2009
First published 2009
ISBN 978 1 84427 390 4

Scripture Union
207–209 Queensway, Bletchley, Milton Keynes, MK2 2EB
Email: info@scriptureunion.org.uk
Website: www.scriptureunion.org.uk

Scripture Union Australia
Locked Bag 2, Central Coast Business Centre, NSW 2252
Website: www.scriptureunion.org.au

Scripture Union USA
PO Box 987, Valley Forge, PA 19482
Website: www.scriptureunion.org

All rights reserved. No part of this publication may be reproduced, stored in a retrieval system, or transmitted in any form or by any means, electronic, mechanical, photocopying, recording or otherwise, without the prior permission of Scripture Union.

The right of Dave Godfrey to be identified as the author of this work has been asserted by him in accordance with the Copyright, Designs and Patents Act 1988.

Scripture quotations are from the Contemporary English Version published by HarperCollinsPublishers © 1991, 1992, 1995 American Bible Society.

British Library Cataloguing-in-Publication Data
A catalogue record of this book is available from the British Library.

Printed and bound in Singapore by Tien Wah Press

Cover and internal design: kwgraphicdesign
Cover and internal illustrations: Craig Cameron

Scripture Union is an international charity working with churches in more than 130 countries, providing resources to bring the good news of Jesus Christ to children, young people and families and to encourage them to develop spiritually through the Bible and prayer.

As well as our network of volunteers, staff and associates who run holidays, church-based events and school Christian groups, we produce a wide range of publications and support those who use our resources through training programmes.

For Emily, Louise, Richard and Robert.

May you find your place in the history of God's people.

Dave Godfrey is an experienced primary teacher and Christian schools worker from York. He travels across the UK training children's leaders and providing events for local churches. He is heavily involved with Spring Harvest, where he leads one of the programmes for 8- to 11-year-olds. He has written and recorded seven albums of children's praise and worship songs including:

Zoom (2007)   *Amazing* (2009)

Dave has also written over 80 songs to help with the teaching of Primary Mathematics. As part of his Number Fun work, he travels across England to train teachers and work in schools.

For further information on his ministry or to order some of his music, you can contact him on:
Telephone: 01904 778848
Fax: 01904 700778
Email: dave@omegazone.org.uk
Websites: www.omegazone.org.uk
          www.numberfun.co.uk
or write to:
PO Box 94, Copmanthorpe, York, YO23 3WW

contents

Introduction

Rocky's Plaice is a five-day children's holiday club. The club is based in a fish and chip restaurant that happens to be the meeting place of a church that loves helping children learn about Jesus! When this cafe church was established, the building was renamed *Rocky's Plaice* in honour of Jesus' friend Peter! The holiday club celebrates the stories of how God established the first ever churches and the life of the church today.

This resource is packed with creative teaching, game, song, prayer and craft ideas. It also contains drama scripts and puppet scripts. *Rocky's Plaice* has a mixture of small group activities and upfront presentations. The material includes two Sunday services, one designed to launch a holiday club and one to round it off.

Rocky's Plaice is written for use with children between the ages of 5 and 11, and is designed to be fast-moving, creative and fun, with a strong teaching element to it.

Rocky's Plaice has been written especially for use with children with little or no church background. It is a tool for churches whose desire is to engage in mission to the children and families in their local area. It should also work equally well for churches wishing to create an atmosphere of discipleship for children already part of the church family.

Rocky's Plaice DVD

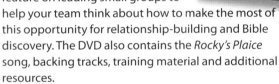

Join Rocky as he prepares a story for the children who come to the Chip Shop Church. Each day he manages to lose his notes, but the visitors to his chip shop manage to help him out just in time! Use the training feature on leading small groups to help your team think about how to make the most of this opportunity for relationship-building and Bible discovery. The DVD also contains the *Rocky's Plaice* song, backing tracks, training material and additional resources.

Rocky's Menu

This 48-page booklet contains all the key Bible text taken from the Contemporary English Version, along with extra information, puzzles and material to use in small groups. It is ideal for use with 8 to 11s. *Daily Specials* for under-8s are also available in the book (as well as on the DVD and the website). They can be used in the small-group sessions or be taken home. Both *Rocky's Menu* and *Daily Specials* help maintain contact with children's homes and act as a reminder, in the weeks after the club, of what the children experienced at *Rocky's Plaice*.

More information on these and other resources can be found on the inside front cover. For all details of the publicity materials produced by CPO, see the inside back cover. (Please note, CPO resources are not available through Scripture Union.)

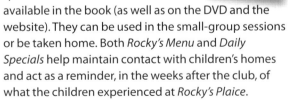

ROCKY'S PLAICE TERMINOLOGY

The Maitre D'

The main presenter of the *Rocky's Plaice* holiday club. (This role has been written for one person to fulfil, but could easily be split between two people.) The Maitre D' (short for maître d'hôtel, in the orignial French, literally 'master of the hotel') in a suitably staffed restaurant or hotel is the person in charge of assigning customers to tables in the establishment and dividing the dining area into areas of responsibility for the various servers on duty.

The Sardines

The music group.

Guest Groups

The small groups that the children will be part of. Activities in Guest Groups include refreshments, Bible reading, listening and prayer, games and craft.

Guest Group Leader

Leader of a Guest Group.

A table for you?

Time to welcome children to their Guest Groups.

Red hot!

Time together for warm-up, telling the story, songs and games.

Ice cream crazy

Small-group time with Bible discovery, refreshments, games and craft.

Extra meaty!

Includes drama, interview, Learn and remember verse and songs.

Get your coats

Small-group time to finish the session.

VISIT THE ROCKY'S PLAICE WEBSITE
To access downloadable versions of the photocopiable resources and other useful material, go to **www.scriptureunion.org. uk/rockysplaice**. You can also read about other people's experiences and check out the advice given by other users on the message boards.

First course Introducing *Rocky's Plaice*

Opening the restaurant

The aims of Rocky's Plaice

Rocky's Plaice is based around the character of Peter and the stories of the early church. Each day we meet Peter and another key character from these early days of the church, who retell their amazing stories. Together with the children we will learn what it means to be part of Jesus' chosen people. **Set menu 5** includes suggestions for a Cornelius party, where the children 'tell' others about what God has done, as Peter told Cornelius.

Rocky's Plaice aims to:

- Tell the amazing story of how God established the first Christian churches
- Help children understand the key concepts that characterised the early Christian church
- Invite children to follow Jesus and to become an active part of his body, the church.
- Provide a fast-moving, fun and action-packed holiday club programme.

THEME AND SETTING

Rocky's Plaice, as the name suggests, is the name of the fish and chip restaurant – a cafe church! If you wanted to pretend that *Rocky's Plaice* is actually in first-century Jerusalem, you could imagine that the room upstairs was the location of the Last Supper and the coming of the Holy Spirit at Pentecost. This might provide a creative link to the story in **Set menu 2**.

Your venue needs to be transformed into a cafe/restaurant setting, with suitable decoration. The venue

can become increasingly decorated throughout the week as you prepare for the party in **Set menu 5**. The restaurant theme is picked up in different ways through this material:

- Peter meets another Bible character each day in the restaurant to tell the stories of the early church.
- There is a special 'fish of the day' which is linked to each day's theme.
- In the dramas we follow the mayhem caused by two trainee chefs who have just joined the kitchens at *Rocky's Plaice*.
- There is the *Rocky's Plaice* theme song and other theme-related games and activities.

The teaching programme

The book of Acts is one of the most exciting books in the Bible. At the beginning of the book we see the early disciples knocked sideways by the death of Jesus, only to be overjoyed at his resurrection. Luke records for us pivotal stories where God intervened in church history, that lead to the world being turned upside down: the story of the Ascension, the story of Pentecost, the healing of the man who couldn't walk and the stories of Dorcas and Cornelius.

Each day has a key word that sums up the themes within the story. In addition, there is an object taken each day from a story chest, to give children a further reminder of the day's story and what it all means. You could pretend that when the church that meets in *Rocky's Plaice* was first established, the people who helped start the church gave the people there a special story chest. This story chest was found whilst tidying up the restaurant in preparation for the holiday club and is full of special objects that helped the first members of *Rocky's Plaice* remember the stories of the early church. The objects, along with the key words written upon them, provide a creative link to the story each day.

The teaching centres on the character and experiences of Peter. Each day one member of the team pretends to be Peter, who, with the help of another early Christian and the day's object from the story chest, retells an amazing story. We will sense the excitement and rapid growth of the early church as God powerfully moved in the lives of his people. It's a story of God at work! Through it we will also understand something of the character of the first Christians as they endeavoured to live out their faith in Jesus.

The *Rocky's Plaice* theme song will help the children remember these key concepts as we build up a picture of the church that met in *Rocky's Plaice*.

The most important section of *Rocky's Plaice* is its teaching programme. It should be well planned, prayed through, prepared properly and presented clearly. The programme will help the children see God in action and challenge them to follow Jesus, just like the early disciples did 2,000 years ago.

Alongside this is the importance of how you relate to the children, as this gives the Bible teaching credibility. Jesus said, 'When you welcome even a child because of me, you welcome me. And when you welcome me, you welcome the one who sent me' (Luke 9:48). So as you welcome children you welcome Jesus; as you talk with them, listen to their stories, laugh at their jokes and cheer their successes. However ordinary they may be, you are doing these things as if to Jesus. Treat them with the love, respect and dignity with which you would honour him.

Rocky's Plaice covers seven days: five 'holiday club' days and two Sunday services. If you are running a club which is shorter, go to the *Rocky's Plaice* website to check out how to adapt the material for three or four days.

Special menu A: Catching the fish
- **Key story:** Peter, Jesus and the breakfast on the beach – John 21:1–19
- **Key theme:** Jesus loves forgiving, Jesus called Peter to help lead the early church.
- **Peter:** Peter retells how he was forgiven for his betrayal of Jesus and given the responsibility of

leading and caring for the early church.
- **Key points:** Jesus' people are a forgiven people, called to love and serve God together. We look forward to the holiday club and set the scene for the week's activities.
- **Key verse:** John 21:16

Set menu 1: Ascension
- **Key word:** Hope
- **Key story:** The Ascension – Acts 1:1–11
- **Key theme:** Jesus is coming back one day.
- **Peter:** Peter meets James in *Rocky's Plaice* and they retell the story of the Ascension. They reveal how this story filled them with hope!
- **Key points:** This day helps set the scene for the coming days. It includes a brief recap of Jesus' life, death and resurrection. Jesus gives the disciples hope of his return and the coming of God's Holy Spirit. Jesus gives people hope, even when things are tough.
- **Key verse:** Acts 1:11

Set menu 2: Pentecost
- **Key word:** Be filled
- **Key story:** Pentecost – Acts 2:1–17
- **Key theme:** Jesus offers the Holy Spirit to his followers.
- **Peter:** Peter meets Priscilla in *Rocky's Plaice* and they retell the story of the Day of Pentecost. They explore what it felt like to be filled with the Holy Spirit for the first time!
- **Key points:** Peter received the power that God promised. The church was born! This day contains an introduction to who God the Holy Spirit is, and that he loves filling his people with power to live for him.
- **Key verse:** Acts 2:39

Set menu 3: The man who couldn't walk
- **Key word:** Have faith
- **Key story:** Peter and John heal a man who couldn't walk – Acts 3:1–21 (and John 3:16)
- **Key theme:** Having faith in Jesus brings eternal life.
- **Peter:** Peter meets John in *Rocky's Plaice* and they retell the story of the day God used them to heal a man who couldn't walk. They recount how it gave them a great opportunity to tell the people around them the good news!
- **Key points:** The good news about Jesus is for all people, including the children in *Rocky's Plaice*. The session includes a section on how Jesus died so we might be forgiven.
- **Key verse:** Acts 3:19

Set menu 4: Dorcas

- **Key word:** Love
- **Key story:** The story of Dorcas – Acts 9:36–43
- **Key theme:** Jesus' followers should be a loving, caring community who reach out in love.
- **Peter:** Peter meets Dorcas in *Rocky's Plaice* and they retell the story of how she loved people because she loved God.
- **Key points:** Jesus loves people! Jesus' command to love other people became a major priority for the early church. God wants us to show his love to the world by loving the people around us.
- **Key verse:** Acts 9:36

Set menu 5: Cornelius

- **Key word:** Tell
- **Key story:** The story of Cornelius – Acts 10:1–29,34,44,45
- **Key theme:** Jesus followers are called to tell the world about Jesus!
- **Peter:** Peter meets Cornelius in *Rocky's Plaice* and they retell the story of how God sent Peter to Cornelius so he, and subsequently people across the world, could discover the good news.
- **Key points:** The Church and the good news is for everyone. This story is a pivotal moment in church history as the message of Jesus went to the non-Jews for the first time.
- **Key verse:** Acts 10:34,35

Special menu B: Breaking out!

- **Key story:** The prayer meeting and the prison break – Acts 12:1–19
- **Key theme:** Jesus call his people to pray and to expect God to answer their prayers.
- **Peter:** Peter meets Rhoda in *Rocky's Plaice* and they retell the story of Peter's escape from prison and the prayer meeting at the house where Rhoda was a servant.
- **Key points:** Jesus loves it when his church prays! A great opportunity to pray for everyone involved in the Holiday Club and to recap on the key themes covered each day.
- **Key verse:** Acts 12:5

A SAMPLE PROGRAMME

This programme runs for 2 hours 30 minutes, not including preparation and clear-up time (2 hours 15 minutes of planned activities and 15 minutes spare for moving around, over-running activities etc).

ACTIVITY	RUNNING TIME	INCLUDES
In the kitchen	*30 minutes*	Spiritual and practical preparation
A table for you? (Small groups)	*10 minutes*	Introductory activities in Guest Groups
Red hot! (All together)	*45 minutes*	Up-front Bible teaching, DVD, warm-up, songs, games, Captain Ketchup
Ice cream crazy (Small groups)	*45 minutes*	Bible discovery, craft, games, refreshments
Extra meaty (All together)	*25 minutes*	Teaching reinforcement, interview, songs, drama, learn and remember verse
Get your coats (Small groups)	*10 minutes*	Creative prayer, reflection
Team clear-up	*30 minutes*	Clearing up, debrief, preparation for the next session

Programme breakdown

Each day's programme contains the following elements:

IN THE KITCHEN

Any holiday club's success must be built on prayer. The material provides notes to encourage the team to think and personally reflect on each day's story from Acts. Before the children arrive, spend some time engaging with the Bible, pray for each other and pray for the children who will meet God through his Word.

During this time, you'll also need to check that you have everything you need for the session (the equipment checklist for each day is a useful way of doing this), make health and safety checks and ensure everything is ready for the children's arrival.

ARRIVING AT *ROCKY'S PLAICE*

The first moments at *Rocky's Plaice* are so important! Be welcoming, but not overwhelming, in putting the children and accompanying adults at their ease. Strike a balance between helping parents to see that their children will be safe with you and giving children a sense of the fun that they'll have during the session. Make sure you have enough people at the registration desk (especially on the first day) to show children and their parents to the right groups. It's always helpful to have someone available to answer questions as the parents leave, or to remind them of the collection time, or just to say a cheerful, 'See you later!'

REGISTRATION

Make sure that the registration desk is well organised with spare forms and pens for any parents who want to register their children at the door. Have a floor plan of your venue to show where each team is sited, so that parents can find their way round. If possible, have a large plan available a little distance away from the desk so that parents dropping children at more than one group can go back to check the layout without clogging up the registration area.

Even if you are keeping central registers with the desk team, Guest Group Leaders will need a copy of who is in their group each day. They should keep these with them at all times, so that in the event of a fire, they can quickly check their team and be sure everyone is safely out of the building.

A TABLE FOR YOU

This time is not just a fill-in until the last child arrives. During this group time, the key aims will be team building and feedback. It is a great time to check out who can remember the memory verse and the key words for each day. Each day there is an introductory activity to do together, during which you can catch up on what the children think and feel about the club. Any children bringing pictures or jokes for the Deep Fat Fryer should be encouraged to put them in the Deep Fat Fryer's chip pan as they arrive.

RED HOT!

This section of the programme is designed to be fast-moving and fun. It contains the main teaching for the day and other elements outlined below. During this period of time, the children are all together for activities led from the front. It includes:

Restaurant cleaning crew

This is an aerobic workout – a 'stomp' type routine where the children pretend to clean up *Rocky's Plaice*, ready for the day. Any fast, lively music could be used, or a special restaurant cleaning crew song is available at http://www.omegazone.org.uk/shop/rockys_plaice.htm. It gives the children a chance to stretch their muscles in a fun way. Be aware of any children with special needs and include some actions that will be easy for them. This section always works best when it has been well prepared.

Key word and story chest

The special object from the story chest is introduced, along with the key word for the day, right at the beginning of the programme. As well as setting the theme for the day, the key word and object will help the children to link the various sections of the programme together in their minds. Each object should have the key word sown, written, marked or painted onto it, or attached in some other way.

Fish of the day

This is a fun introduction to the theme of the day. Each day a fish is presented on the screen and a link is made to the key word for the day.

Mega game

This is a short screen-based team game. Each day's game is slightly different and details are given in the programme outline. Due to the high-speed nature of these short games, it usually works best if the children call out the answers and the Guest Group Leader takes notes. The Maitre D' then quickly reveals the answers to the challenge, with the leaders marking their team's sheets. Award points for correct answers. If no point system is in operation, declare the group with the most correct answers, 'Mega Game Champions' for the day. See the *Rocky's Plaice* website for some ideas about running a points system through the week.

Singing

Children enjoy singing and learning new songs. Choose a mix of songs that children who come to your church regularly will know and songs that are new to everyone. If you have children who are not used to church, avoid songs that express belief or faith and keep them factual ('God is' or 'Jesus did' rather than 'I believe'). The *Rocky's Plaice* theme song is the theme for the week, so sing that a couple of times during the whole session.

Red Hot News

The Red Hot News is read by Captain Ketchup. Captain Ketchup can either be a person live on stage, or a puppet presenting from behind a puppet screen. This superhero's job is to help the children 'ketch-up' on the previous day's storyline, and introduce the arrival of Peter into *Rocky's Plaice*. Captain Ketchup puppets are available by special request from One Way UK (go to **www. onewayuk.com**). If the character is played by an adult, then they should wear as much red as possible, including a big red cape. A logo and special Captain Ketchup song are available from **www.omegazone.org.uk/shop**

Storytelling

Each day, one leader pretends to be Peter and another pretends to be his special guest. Together they present the story for the day. Each actor should come to the front dressed in a suitable costume and, where possible, act out the story in front of the children as they tell it. It is best if each actor has learnt the script, as this enables them to communicate effectively to the children, adding as much personal experience, feelings and emotion as possible.

The *Rocky's Plaice* DVD has five storytelling episodes to help retell the Bible story. If you don't have strong storytellers, you may choose to use the DVD as the primary storytelling tool. Alternatively, you might choose to do the live action retelling, and reinforce the story using the DVD. See page 4 for more details of the DVD.

Maitre D's recommendations

This is where the Maitre D' brings the thoughts of the children and the storyteller together and relates them to the key word for the day. Don't labour this section,

but make it punchy and to the point. It's important that you choose a good communicator to deliver this section: someone who can really connect with the children and open up the stories simply and clearly. This section helps the children see how the teaching applies to them – it should leave them thinking and challenged!

ICE CREAM CRAZY

The children move into their Guest Groups for their refreshments, Bible exploration, craft and games. You can choose to do the craft and games in Guest Groups, or all together. It depends on what team and facilities you have. Guest Groups are a crucial time for relationship building.

Refreshment zone

Be creative in providing refreshments. Try making shaped biscuits (fish, chips etc) or other theme related goodies. This section should allow the children to have a drink and go to the toilet, and be ready to unroll the scrolls.

Luke's scrolls

This time allows children to develop skills in thinking about the meaning of the Bible and how it applies to their life. The Bible exploration can be done using *Rocky's Menu* or *Daily Specials*, through discussions using flip-chart paper and pens, or a combination of both. Photocopiable notes for each Guest Group Leader are available on page 45–47. Make sure all Guest Group Leaders are prepared for these important times. For training on running a small group, see the training section on page 20 or the feature on the *Rocky's Plaice* DVD.

Craft and games

Craft and games for use during *Rocky's Plaice* can be found on page 27–29. For further inspiration, see *Ultimate Craft* and *Ultimate Games* which each contain hundreds of ideas that might be suitable for your club.

Make sure you risk assess these activities, and collect all the necessary materials. These times provide a good opportunity for leaders and children to chat and build relationships.

Ultimate Craft
£12.99, 978 1 84427 364 5

Ultimate Games
£9.99, 978 1 84427 365 2

EXTRA MEATY!

During this period of time the children are all together for activities led from the front.

The sizzler

As the different groups return from their various activities, a 'Sizzler' is put up on screen – this is a key question that focuses the children's thoughts back to the main teaching point of the day. This should be discussed in groups and the Maitre D' should get some feedback from children/leaders, before going on to recap the main learning objective. This will help the children to understand and process the teaching presented and discussed during the morning. It should take no longer than five minutes and should be visual and interactive.

Deep Fat Fryer

The Deep Fat Fryer is a leader dressed in a monk costume, who is responsible for collecting and presenting some of the jokes and pictures that have been put in his (clean!) chip pan. He also introduces everyone to the restaurant dog called Scraps, who is unable to meet the children each day due to various mishaps. The children are encouraged to draw pictures of Scraps and put them in the Deep Fat Fryer's chip pan.

Totally meaty Learn and remember verse

Each day, the children will be challenged to continue learning the verse for the week (John 3:16). A different activity is given each day to learn the verse. A Learn and remember verse song is available on the *Rocky's Plaice* DVD (the lyrics and sheet music are also available on the *Rocky's Plaice* website).

Dish of the Day

Each day, a member of the team is interviewed about following Jesus, focusing on the theme for the day. It gives an opportunity for the children to discover how the Bible teaching relates to everyday life for those who follow Jesus. Not everything that God does in people's lives is appropriate for children so choose testimonies with care. If possible, encourage the children to come up with questions they'd like to ask the Dish of the Day and put them in the Deep Fat Fryer's chip pan.

Drama: The Adventures of Salt and Vinegar

Salt and Vinegar are two trainee chefs who have just begun working at *Rocky's Plaice*. As children watch Salt and Vinegar in their messy quest to become Super Star Chefs, they might notice a link to each key word for the day. The drama is not designed to be a primary teaching tool, but a reinforcement of the theme and a lot of slapstick fun! The scripts are slightly longer than those in previous SU programmes. However, they can be cut down by missing out elements such as Salt and Vinegar's song, if you have limited time during the session (or limited rehearsal time).

Extra meaty finale!

This wraps up the all-together time with the *Rocky's Plaice* theme song, and maybe another song the children have enjoyed. Include here a prayer too, thanking God for your time together today.

GET YOUR COATS

The session draws to a close in small groups. This part of the programme allows the children to make their own personal response to what they have learnt. It includes ideas for creative prayer and 'now' response times where questions can be raised in a safe and positive environment.

Guest Group Leaders should make a point of saying goodbye and reminding children of the next session.

TEAM CLEAR-UP

It may be that some of the team have their own children at *Rocky's Plaice* and are unable to stay for long when the programme ends. As a minimum, have everyone together to check any problems, briefly remind people of tomorrow's activities and pray for the Holy Spirit to be at work in the children.

If you have the time and the facilities, the team could share lunch together to round off the time together.

Other elements of Rocky's Plaice

SERVICES

Starting *Rocky's Plaice* with a church service the Sunday before a club is a good way of getting the church praying for the club and commissioning the leaders. A service after the club will round things off nicely and be a good event to invite parents to. Outlines for these services are on page 53 and 89. Research has shown that if you include the services in the dates of your club, then more children and families will attend them. So, instead of calling your club a five-day programme call it a seven-day club! This is a good way of welcoming families with no church background into your community.

UNDER-5s RESOURCES

For details of resources to use with 5s and under, visit the *Rocky's Plaice* website. The resources follow the same Bible passages and themes as the main programme.

11 TO 14s RESOURCES

For details of resources to use with 11 to 14s, visit the *Rocky's Plaice* website. The resources follow the same Bible passages and themes as the main programme.

14 TO 18s – YOUNG LEADERS

Having young people help out at a holiday club is a fantastic way of discipling and training them in leadership. For training materials for use specifically with 14 to 18s in leadership, go to the *Rocky's Plaice* website.

CORNELIUS PARTY

In **Set menu 5**, there is a party feel to the session, as children celebrate *Rocky's Plaice* and what God has done in the stories they have heard during the club. You could also include the families of the children in your club by putting on a family event – a Cornelius party – where the children tell their families about the events of *Rocky's Plaice* and what they have learnt. This could be on the Friday evening or Saturday after the club (this would enable you to invite families again to the Sunday service following the club). Put together a programme of games and craft (from the *Rocky's Plaice* programme, together with some new ones) and activities that families can do together. Set aside part of your venue to be a cafe area for parents to take time out of the programme and make sure there are team members to chat to there.

OTHER FAMILY ACTIVITIES

Following the food theme, barbeques and picnics are a great opportunity to invite families (indeed, these could form part of your Cornelius party). Get the whole church involved in organising the food or running activities. Make sure you invite families new to your community to other events.

DADS AND LADS/MUMS AND DAUGHTERS

Sometimes single-sex events give more flexibility and you can tailor the programme a bit more. For example, pampering evenings for mums and daughters or a gadgets night for dads and lads can prove effective relationship-building times.

AUTHOR'S RESOURCES

Dave Godfrey, the author of *Rocky's Plaice,* has some extra resources available at http://www.omegazone. org.uk/shop/rockys_plaice.htm. These include the Cleaning Crew and Captain Ketchup songs, together with PowerPoints to be used during the up front sessions. If you want a set of songs to use and repeat throughout your holiday club, Dave recommends the following from two of his albums:

'Zoom' album
Children of Courage
What is your God like?
Praising

'Amazing' album
Amazing!
I can't run enough
Cheese
The Sat Nav song

Following up Rocky's Plaice

A holiday club only lasts a short time, but what about the rest of the year? How will you and your church community stay in touch with those children and families who have no other connection with church, apart from the holiday club? Planning follow-up is as vital as planning the club itself. See page 92 for great ideas on what you can do through the rest of the year. Maybe you could start a midweek club (see page 93 for details of *Take Away*, a follow-up midweek club programme to *Rocky's Plaice*). You could build up links with your local primary schools by offering to take assemblies or give out copies of *It's Your Move!* to Year-6 children as they move on to secondary school. For ideas and advice, contact Scripture Union on 01908 856170 or your local schools work trust.

Second course Setting up a holiday club
Deciding the menu

Planning Rocky's Plaice

When starting to think about running a holiday club, some big issues need to be tackled:

DEFINE YOUR AIMS

The broad aims of *Rocky's Plaice* are on page 6, but each individual holiday club will have its own specific aims. *Rocky's Plaice* can provide a manageable, creative and fun way of reaching out to the children of your neighbourhood with the good news of Jesus. It can provide an excellent opportunity to blow any misconceptions away and to reveal to them a God who loves them passionately.

Here are some aims which you might choose for your club:

- To attract new children to join your Sunday groups or other children's activities.
- To develop your leaders' gifts and experience.
- To present the gospel to children who've never heard it.
- To provide an opportunity for children to make an initial or further commitment to follow Jesus.
- To get to know the children in your church.
- To provide a project to encourage your church to work together.
- To establish links with the children's families.
- To encourage cooperation with other churches or groups in your area.
- To launch an ongoing children's group based on the *Rocky's Plaice* theme.
- To give parents a few mornings off in the school holidays.

Any or all of these aims may be appropriate, but you'll have to decide what you want *Rocky's Plaice* to achieve in your situation. If you have several aims, you'll need to decide which are the most important. You'll also need to evaluate *Rocky's Plaice* afterwards, to see if you met your aims. Decide now how you'll do that. How will you measure success? Try the aims form on the *Rocky's Plaice* website or DVD to focus your aims and help the rest of your team buy into the aims you have set.

THE CHILDREN

Once you have set your aims, you'll be able to make other key decisions such as:

Who will you invite to Rocky's Plaice?

Do your aims relate to the children already involved in your church, or those outside it?

How many children do you want to involve? If your main aim is to get to know the children better, you might need to restrict numbers. On the other hand, if you want to present the gospel to children who haven't heard it, you may want as many as possible to attend.

What age range(s) do you want to target with *Rocky's Plaice*? Do you want to cater for an age range that is well represented in your groups, or one that isn't? Will you be able to tailor the activities in a way that will appeal to a wide age range? *Rocky's Plaice* is designed for use with children between the ages of 5 and 11. See page 12 for information on where to find resources to use with other age groups.

When will you run your club, and for how long?

You'll need to fix the date for your holiday club early enough for people to take it into account when they book their holidays. It is also essential that the dates do not clash with other holiday clubs in the area, activities already booked at your premises, holidays organised by local schools, holidays/camps for local Boys' Brigade, Girls' Brigade, Cub or Brownie groups, and carnivals or local events taking place in your area.

The potential leaders' availability will have the most effect on the duration of your holiday club. If most of your leaders need to take time off work, it may not be practical to run a full five-day club.

If you are planning to run your club over three or four days, rather than five, go to the *Rocky's Plaice* website (**www.scriptureunion.org.uk/rockysplaice**) for guidance on how to adapt the material for a shorter club.

LEGAL REQUIREMENTS

There are various legal requirements you will need to be familiar with and conform to as you prepare for your holiday club. These include having a child protection policy in place, providing adequate space in your venue, meeting adult to child ratios, insurance. To obtain up-to-date information on all of these requirements, go to the *Rocky's Plaice* website.

FINANCES

You'll need to consider your financial resources. Work out what you'll need money for. Examples might include:

- craft materials
- refreshments
- materials for the scenery
- photocopying/printing costs
- hire of premises
- hire of equipment such as a video projector
- *Rocky's Plaice* resource books for your leaders
- resources such as the *Rocky's Plaice* DVD and *Rocky's Menu*
- prizes or presents for the children

Do you need to do some fund-raising? Or will you charge a small fee for children to attend *Rocky's Plaice*? Research shows that in many cases, making a charge for a club has no effect on the number of children who come. Indeed, some parents may value a club they have had to pay for more highly than something that is free.

PUBLICITY

The best way to ensure you have plenty of children at your holiday club is for the event to be well publicised. There is material available from CPO to help you with

this. See the inside back cover for details. Here are some things to consider:

Posters and flyers
Use these to advertise *Rocky's Plaice*.

Letters and forms
How about sending a letter or invitation card to every child your church has contact with? Or you might distribute letters to all the children in your area, maybe through the local schools. Your letter could enclose an application/registration form to be returned to you. You may also need a follow-up letter, which will enclose a consent/medical form, and perhaps a *Rocky's Plaice* badge.

School assemblies
You may have a local Christian schools worker, or people from your church who are involved in schools ministry. Or you may have some church members who are teachers. If so, they could promote your *Rocky's Plaice* event in a school assembly, if the school is happy for them to do so.

Press releases
Holiday clubs provide the kind of story that local papers love to cover. By getting a story in the press, you'll increase the appeal of your holiday club and show that the church(es) involved are reaching out into your local community. By mentioning Scripture Union's name it increases our awareness, which ultimately allows us to improve resources like our holiday club material. If you have a good relationship with your local press, then make contact in the usual way and inform them of your event. If this is something you have never considered, a press release template is available on the *Rocky's Plaice* website. Include your club's details and send the press release to your local paper.

Prayer cards/bookmarks
It is important to keep your church informed about your event. Prayer cards or prayer bookmarks can help your church members pray for your holiday club – before, during and after your *Rocky's Plaice* event.

PLAN IN DETAIL

In the few months before *Rocky's Plaice*, you'll need to consider and organise the following aspects.

Presentation and teaching
How will you adapt the material to suit your particular age group(s)? What audio/visual aids will you need? Will you need amplification or video projection equipment? Who will be the Maitre D'? Will you need more than one main presenter?

Programme priorities

You may not have time to fit in all the activities that are suggested. Within Guest Group times, especially during Ice cream crazy, you could get so engrossed in general conversation that you never start on the Bible discussions, so be sure to plan carefully.

Imagine filling a jar up to the top with pebbles. You might think it is now full, but try adding some smaller stones and you'll find there is room for them. Is it full now? Try pouring in water, and you will see that only then is the jar really full. But if you put in this amount of either small stones or water first you would not then get everything in! When planning, make sure you put in the essentials first – upfront Bible teaching and discussion time in groups. Then add the less vital but still important things, and finally the parts that 'fill it up'.

Music

Choose the songs for the week, and gather the musicians together to rehearse them. It's good to have a number of musicians playing a variety of instruments, but you'll need to make sure you have enough stage space for other things too! Choose a few new songs and a few old favourites. Make sure you include non-confessional songs, so that the children are not singing words they might not believe. If you don't have musicians in your team, you could use backing tracks or simply sing along to a CD/MP3.

Drama

Do you need to adapt the script to fit the number or gender of your cast members, or the limitations of your venue? How much rehearsal time will you need? How will you obtain or make the necessary props, costumes and scenery?

Training

Undertaking some basic skills and knowledge training is vital for the success of the holiday club. You should aim to have at least two sessions together in preparation, and you should ensure that these are more or less compulsory for team members. As part of these sessions, the vision and practicalities of *Rocky's Plaice* can also be outlined. Training is outlined in the Third course.

Ice cream crazy

You'll need to think about how you are going to stage this small-groups/craft/games time. What you do depends on your aims and the resources you have available.

- You could have every Guest Group doing the same activity on the same day. This means that only one simple explanation from the front is needed, and group leaders can help each other. It also helps to develop relationships within the Guest Groups. This does, however, require a lot of resources, and activities which suit this format are limited.
- Alternatively, you could set up activities for the whole week and children rotate around these activities. This means fewer resources are needed for each activity, more activities are possible, and different leaders can take responsibility for leading the same activity each day. However, it is harder to theme each activity to the day's teaching. Some groups will not have their Guest Group Leader with them during this time if they are leading another activity. You will probably also need specific areas that can be dedicated to each activity, and your venue may not be large enough.

Craft

Where will you get the necessary materials and equipment? Do you need to ask your congregation to collect particular items? A dedicated craft team can be very useful, especially in the run-up to *Rocky's Plaice*. This team should collect the necessary materials etc. They'll also be able to make templates and patterns for the children to draw around or cut out. The craft team should make up prototypes of the craft, and pass on any hints to the Guest Group Leaders.

Involve local schools in amassing reusable material to use during the week (glass jars, plastic bottles, travel magazines for collage etc). This gets people actively contributing to the club before it has begun, including the children!

Games

Consider what games you can play based on the number of children, your venue and the equipment you have. Make sure you have all the equipment you need.

Data protection

How will you maintain the confidentiality of the information you receive on the registration forms? Make sure your church is registered under the Data Protection Act. Visit www.informationcommissioner. gov.uk and click on 'Data protection'.

Accidents

Make sure you have at least one person appointed as a first-aider with a current first aid certificate and access to an up-to-date first aid kit. The whole team should know who is responsible for first aid. You will also need an accident book to record any incidents. This is essential in the event of an insurance claim. The matter should be recorded, however small, along with details of the action taken. For other health and safety information visit **www.rospa.co.uk**

Fire procedures

It is essential that the whole team knows emergency procedures, including fire exits and assembly points, and where to access a telephone in case of emergency. Ensure you keep all fire exits clear.

Prayer team

Make sure you have a team of people committed to pray throughout the preparation and the club itself. Keep the whole church well informed too. The prayer team should keep on praying for the children in the club in the months after *Rocky's Plaice* finishes.

Use of the Bible

One of the aims of *Rocky's Plaice* is to help children read the Bible for themselves. So each day during Ice cream crazy, when you move on to discussing the passage, help them find it in the Bible or *Rocky's Menu* and learn to look for answers there. Use a translation that is easy for children to read (Good News Bible, Contemporary English Version or International Children's Bible).

SET THE SCENE

Choosing a venue is a very important issue. Sometimes a community hall or school is a well-equipped, neutral venue that can be non-threatening for children and parents outside the church. However, you may wish to use this opportunity to introduce the children and parents to your church building. This can also help save on the cost of hiring an alternative venue. The venue does need to have enough space for the number of children and the type of activities you are planning. You will need access to the venue before the holiday club to ensure the necessary preparations can be made.

Setting up the room

The holiday club will be greatly enhanced if the main room you are using is transformed into a lively fish and chip restaurant! This will help create a wonderful atmosphere and spark the children's imagination. You will need to think creatively about how you can transform your venue into an exciting place. The creative use of cardboard, wood, paint and other materials can make a real difference. Think creatively about what you can hang from the ceiling, cover the walls with and put on the floor. It may be that someone in your area has already done *Rocky's Plaice* and has scenery and decorations you could borrow. Go to **www.scriptureunion.org.uk/rockysplaice** and click on 'Bulletin board'.

To transform the area you could:

- Cover the walls with big pictures of fish (each small group could have a massive fish in their team colour next to their Guest Group location in the room).
- Ask all the Refreshment team to wear chef's costumes.
- Decorate the hall with multicoloured bunting.
- Make giant menu cards to stick around the walls.
- Use plastic check tablecloths in each Guest Group location either on the floor or on tables.
- If you have windowsills or other suitable surfaces in your location you could put plastic flowers in jam jars on them.

The stage area

You will need a focal point at the front from which the Maitre D' can run the programme. Create a Red Hot News desk area on one side of the stage. Think about where you will do your dramas and where the band will be positioned. You will also need to decide where the projection screen should be located. A draped-off area or an attached room needs to be provided for the actors in the drama to come out of. Alternatively they could appear from behind Captain Ketchup's puppet screen. The boundary for the stage area could be marked by a masking tape line across the floor.

Guest Group locations

The rest of the room can be split up into Guest Group locations. Colour-coding the locations would help the children know where their group meets and help bring the venue to life with colour. It may be best to keep chairs out of the way, except for those who cannot sit on the floor, so that the room can be used for the energetic sections of the programme without objects getting in the way. If there is room, having some tables set up for each group would also help it take on a restaurant feel.

Fill the screen

If you are using a video projector or OHP, use a default image when it is not being used, so that the screen is never blank. Use something simple, like the *Rocky's Plaice* logo or some photos of different fish or food. The logo and other artwork are available on the DVD-ROM section of the *Rocky's Plaice* DVD or on the website.

Third course Working with your team
Staff training

DEVELOPING PEOPLE'S POTENTIAL

As well as being a time of great fun and development for the children attending, a holiday club is also an important time for the adults leading and helping out. Helping with a holiday club can be a big step for people in the development of their gifts and ministry.

How does a holiday club develop people's potential?
- It involves people in the church who don't usually work with children.
- It is an opportunity for people of all ages to work together in a way that may not happen at any other time of the year. (A regular comment at one holiday club from team members is, 'This is the best week of the year in church!' It's probably the most demanding and tiring too!).
- It develops people's gifts and lets them take risks.
- It discovers people's untapped gifts and enthusiasms.
- It provides a structure for the overall leadership of the club/church to seek out and encourage people to 'have a go'. (The age of volunteering has passed so don't rely on issuing a general plea for volunteers. Look at who you have available and ask people personally, giving them good reasons why you think they could fulfil whatever task you have identified. That suggests that you believe in them. They are far more likely to agree to get involved!).

AREAS OF RESPONSIBILITY

A successful holiday club requires a variety of support teams to be set up and individuals taking responsibility for different areas of the programme. Listed below are some of the different teams you will need and some of the key roles people will need to assume before, during and after the event. Some people will be able to play more than one role for *Rocky's Plaice*.

Core planning team

All the helpers should be involved in planning and preparing for *Rocky's Plaice*, but you will need a smaller team to coordinate things and make some initial decisions. As well as the holiday club's overall leader, this should include your most experienced leaders, your minister and your children's workers.

Restaurant manager

This is the overall leader, ideally someone who is not involved in the presentation. Their role would be to:
- Make any on-the-spot decisions such as accepting extra children at the door.
- Keep the whole programme to time, moving things on when necessary.
- Look at quality of presentation, watching out for problems such as too much banter between team and Maitre D'.
- Watch out for children who are not joining in well and helping them to become part of things.
- Being the person to whom everyone would report in the event of a fire.

Maitre D'

This is the upfront presenter of the club. There could be two people in this role, and that would lighten the load on any one person. The Maitre D' should be confident on stage and have experience of leading a programme in a fun but flexible manner. They could be dressed as a head waiter! If they are the person doing the teaching application and reinforcement, they will need to be prepared on what they are going to say. (Maitre D' is the name for a head waiter in a restaurant.)

Guest Group Leaders

Each small group needs a leader. This Guest Group Leader should be at the club every day and will be the person with whom the children have the most personal contact. The leader's role is to get to know the children so that they feel welcome and comfortable at *Rocky's Plaice*. The programme is designed to give the Guest Group Leaders enough time in their Guest Groups to have meaningful discussions, including ones that apply the teaching programme to the children's lives.

They should coordinate all small-group activities and sit with their Guest Group during the upfront times. The Guest Group Leader should have a copy of the register, be aware of any special needs and ensure that children all leave safely at the end of the day's session.

Assistant Guest Group Leaders

The role of the Assistant is to support the Guest Group Leader and ideally should also be available every day. This is a good way to develop the leadership skill of young or inexperienced team members.

All team members should be given training in dealing with children, especially in relation to physical contact and not being with children alone out of sight of others, but Guest Group Leaders and Assistants especially need to be aware of child protection issues and policies.

If you have a large holiday club, you may choose to appoint Guest Group coordinators to oversee six or eight Guest Groups who are all in one age range. It is best if these coordinators do not have a group of their own.

Captain Ketchup

Captain Ketchup is either a puppet or a member of the team, who presents the Red Hot News. For more details, see page 10.

The cleaning crew

These people lead a simple aerobic workout each morning to help children expend some energy at the start of the session. They should keep the actions simple, basing them on moves you might do when cleaning. Build up the number of different moves throughout the week, but remember to consider children in your club who have special needs, and include moves that they can do too.

Deep Fat Fryer

A member of the team dressed as a monk, who reads out jokes and shows pictures that children have put in the fryer's (clean!) chip pan. The fryer should look through the items in the chip pan at the end of Ice cream crazy, so that they can pick the ones they are going to use. Try to use as a many contributions as possible (without taking up too much time) and display the pictures and jokes on a board for all the club to see.

Drama team

A small team of three people should take responsibility for the *Rocky's Plaice* drama. These people need to be reasonably confident as actors with the ability to project their voice. The prewritten sketches are somewhat messy and silly and will need some coordination. The team should be willing to learn their lines and to practise each sketch until they can perform it with confidence.

One of the drama team (or another person) needs to take the responsibility of Props Manager, and collect and prepare all the props.

The Sardines (the worship band)

Having a live band can add something special to a holiday club. If you can't use live music, then sing along to a CD. Could The Sardines be creatively dressed?

Printing and publicity team

A small team, including at least one computer-literate person, should take responsibility for all the design, printing and publicity for *Rocky's Plaice*. Your aim should be to produce publicity that is visually impressive, consistent, accurate and attractive.

The publicity will need to be colourful, and use the *Rocky's Plaice* logo (available on the DVD or website), an attractive, child-friendly font, pictures and clip art. The publicity team should take responsibility for:

- Posters and fliers to advertise *Rocky's Plaice*.
- Registration forms for the children to fill in (see sample version on the website).
- Consent forms for parents/guardians/carers (see sample version on the website).
- Invitation cards or letters to go with the appropriate forms.
- Forms for potential team members, including an indication of roles they'd like to take on. You should also send CRB forms out with these forms if the team member has not already had clearance.
- Notes and training materials for the team. Even if someone else writes this material, the printing and publicity team should be responsible for the layout.
- Name badges for the team members and for any adults who are on site and part of *Rocky's Plaice*.
- Signs and notices. These will be needed around the site, including the main hall, entrances, toilets and areas that are out of bounds. These should use the

same typeface and colours as other materials to maintain the consistent *Rocky's Plaice* theme.
- Prayer cards/bookmarks – prayer pointers to help church members to pray for the holiday club before, during and after *Rocky's Plaice* events.

CPO produce a wide range of *Rocky's Plaice* publicity or other merchandise. For details, see the inside back cover.

Registration team
Responsible for:
- Allocation of children to groups.
- Checking children in and out each day.
- Checking forms are completed fully.
- Keeping a check on team sizes if more children register during *Rocky's Plaice*.
- Ensuring each child is to be picked up or has permission to walk home themselves. If you have a lot of children attending the club, it can be hard to keep track of who has permission to collect which child, especially when parents help each other out. A collection slip, which can be given to the adult who will pick the child up, is on the *Rocky's Plaice* website.

If you are advertising the club through a local school or community groups, provide children with booking forms in advance which can be filled out and sent back to the leader of the holiday club, school office or community group leader. This allows you to allocate children to groups in advance and will inform you of dietary requirements, medical issues and physical, educational or behavioural special needs. A register can be made, based on the names and ages provided. A copy of a register must also be given to each group leader in case of a fire or emergency.

In some contexts, pre-registering is not practical, therefore ensure on the first day that there are plenty of volunteers available to help greet the children and their parents or carers and to provide them with the registration form to fill in. Children should not attend the event if permission has not been granted. As this can be a lengthy process, you might like to open the doors earlier on Day 1 and during registration, engage the children in parachute games, upfront games or a short film.

Refreshment team
This team will play a vital role during the week. They will be responsible for:
- Checking with the registration team that you have no children with food allergies.
- Obtaining and preparing the refreshments for the children.

- Tidying up after the refreshments have been given out.

For this team to work efficiently you may like to choose one person to coordinate the group. If you are providing anything more than a drink and a biscuit, you should have someone with a food hygiene certificate. Think about using (recyclable) disposable cups or bottles to save on washing-up time.

Security
The person in charge of security will be responsible for ensuring that no child leaves the building unless they have permission to do so, and that only children or adults who are part of *Rocky's Plaice* are allowed to enter the building.

It is important for each adult to have an appropriate, clearly labelled badge to identify them and their role. The children registered for *Rocky's Plaice* should have their own badge. Any adult or child on site not wearing an appropriate badge should be challenged.

First-aider
Aim to have at least one member of your team with a valid first aid certificate. If possible have assistants too – a male for the boys and a female for the girls. These people will need a current first aid certificate, and access to a first aid kit. You will also need an accident book to record any incidents or accidents. (This is essential in the event of any insurance claim. A record of the matter should be noted, along with details of action taken. It should be countersigned where appropriate.)

Health and safety person
This person will need to plan how you will evacuate the building in the event of a fire. Check that fire escapes are kept clear, that the team know the position of fire extinguishers, and know what the fire alarm – or noise that means 'leave the building immediately' – sounds like. Each Guest Group Leader should be a roll-call marshal for their teams. The health and safety person is in charge of clearing the building and dealing with the emergency services, but they should allocate responsibility for checking other areas of the building (toilets, snack bar etc) to other team members who will be present each day. You may want to incorporate a fire drill into your programme early in the week. The children will be used to this from school, but it might help the adults!

They should also make sure all the activities are adequately risk-assessed before the club starts.

Craft and equipment

Someone should take responsibility for making sure that everything that is needed for the craft, creative prayer and Guest Group activities is in the correct place at the right time. Get as much as possible of the craft prepared in advance; there may well be church members who, while they can't help at the club itself, will be happy to help with cutting out etc.

Try to prepare a finished version of each item to show the children what they are making, and providing everything needed for each team's vanity case (pens, paper, plasticine etc). Each day one of the craft team should explain how the craft is made and supervise the activity, even if it is done in Guest Groups.

Technical manager

The amount of technology used will vary with the size and nature of each club. A technical manager could take responsibility for:

- Visual – OHP or laptop and projector, screen, or DVD and TV.
- Audio – PA for presenters and band, CD/MP3 player.

Training the staff

However experienced your team, there are two key areas to cover in training: good practice in working with children and delivering the *Rocky's Plaice* programme itself. Here is a suggested programme for two training sessions. However, this material could easily be spread over several sessions.

SESSION 1

- **Skills**: Leading a small group (incorporating dealing with challenging behaviour)
- **Skills**: Praying with children
- **Skills**: Reading the Bible with children
- **Understanding**: Working with special needs
- **Understanding**: Working with children from other faith backgrounds

SESSION 2

- **Introduction**: 'God did it' – A Holy Spirit overview
- **Practicalities**: Basic outline of *Rocky's Plaice*, learning the theme song, daily structure etc.
- **Prayer**: For *Rocky's Plaice* and all who come

SESSION 1
WORKING WITH CHILDREN

Welcome

Make sure you give the team a big welcome, ensuring refreshments are freely available, with the *Rocky's Plaice* theme song playing in the background as people arrive. (Alternatively you could serve everyone a fish and chip supper!)

Leading a small group

Leading a small group of children is a vital part of *Rocky's Plaice*. Guest Group Leaders will be the ones who get to know and build relationships with the children. Sometimes these relationships can develop into long-term friendships. Understanding how these groups work and having a set of guidelines are really important.

Small-group role play

If you have a fairly confident group of leaders, try this role play activity. Six or seven leaders play typical children in a group, and one leader is the Guest Group Leader. This small group is going to look at the Luke's Scrolls activity from Set menu 1 (see page 58). Split your team into groups of seven or eight, and make sure you provide enough sets of the character descriptions (see below) and everything that you need for the Luke's Scrolls activity.

Give out the character descriptions and tell the teams not to show anyone their piece of paper, but to act it out during the activity as best they can. Encourage the team not to totally overact and make their group leader's role a total nightmare, but to take it as seriously as they can.

- You are the Guest Group Leader. Your group has lots of needs, and you should try very hard to include everyone in the discussion and keep the discussion on track!
- You are an intelligent child who knows all the answers and keeps putting their hand up to answer, or to ask a question, but you don't call out or interrupt.
- You are a very shy younger child, who will be very slow in interacting with the group.
- You are a fidgeter who can't keep still, yet is following what is being discussed.
- You are a child who naturally interrupts all the time, but should respond to firm handling by your Guest Group Leader. You should ask to go to the toilet at least once during the short group time.
- You are an average sort of child, who is interested in the teaching and discussion. You have got a bit of a crush on your leader, so go and sit next to them if you can and maintain eye contact.

■ You listen well and follow all that your leader asks you do to, making a valuable contribution to the group.

■ You are deeply committed to Jesus and yet find it very difficult to articulate how you feel or what to say. You try very hard to contribute to the group.

Feedback from the role play

The activity should be a good, fun way of raising some of the issues involved in leading a small group. Have some flip-chart paper and markers ready to note down any interesting points to come from the groups.

Talk first to the Guest Group Leaders, encouraging them that at *Rocky's Plaice* it will never be as difficult as the last few minutes! Ask them to outline the characters in their group. What was difficult to deal with? Who contributed? Who didn't contribute and why?

Discuss some of the issues raised by the characters, eg how are you going to handle children going to the toilet? How should you handle leader crushes?

By the time the feedback has finished you should have a set of guidelines for leading a group. Below are a few dos and don'ts which may be worth adding to discussion at the end.

Dos and don'ts of leading a small group

■ Do learn their names and call them by name.

■ Do take notice of how each child behaves, reacts and interacts so you can get to know each one quickly.

■ Do take the initiative. Let them know clearly what you expect from the group, how each one is valued and encouraged to participate in the life of the group.

■ Do be specific in your prompting and questions (this can help everyone contribute).

■ Do try to meet the children's needs (each child will come with their own needs).

■ Don't assume that all the children will learn from or experience the club in the same way.

■ Do be polite and patient (even if one or two children really annoy you!).

■ Do add oodles of enthusiasm to your group (they will pick up on your attitude – you are a role model).

■ Do think creatively eg how you sit, lie or kneel as a group to discuss things.

■ Do model what you expect the children to do, eg response to the stage.

■ Do be careful to follow closely any instructions or notes you are given.

■ Do ask for help if you need it (you are not alone!).

■ Do be careful with language (no jargon, complicated or inappropriate language).

■ Do pray for them and yourself as you lead the group.

■ Don't take favourites.

■ Do not be physical with them (this can be misinterpreted).

Here are a few extra thoughts about keeping control to guide you.

The key to establishing good discipline and control is relationship building and clear expectations – these need to be thought through before *Rocky's Plaice* starts. This can be done by:

■ Setting some ground rules and boundaries for the group – and sticking to them!

■ Having plenty of materials for everyone.

■ Ensuring that you have enough leaders at all times.

■ Positively reinforcing the children's behaviour when they answer or do something well.

■ Never sacrificing the needs of the group for one child.

For more information on leading small groups, check out *Top Tips on Leading small groups*
SU, 978 1 84427 388 1
£2.99

For more information on managing behaviour, see *Top Tips on Handling difficult behaviour*
SU, 978 1 84427 124 5,
£2.99

Praying with children

There will be many chances to pray with children during *Rocky's Plaice*. When you go through the programme in Session 2, make sure your team know when these chances are. There are two different aspects that come up during *Rocky's Plaice*: praying about things with children and helping children make a response.

Praying with children

■ Ask the children to name some of the things they want to pray for.

■ Break these down into things they want to say sorry for, things they want to say thank you to God for, and things they want to ask for themselves or others.

■ If you are going to lead the prayer yourself, make sure that you keep to the point and include the suggestions the children made.

■ Encourage the children, where possible, to lead the prayers with you.

- Be imaginative in using different ways to pray, eg using pictures or objects to stimulate thought; music to help praise or reflection; prayers with a set response; taking it in turns using one sentence; or prayers using different bodily postures. Suggestions are given each day for praying creatively.
- Take care to use simple, clear modern English, free from jargon, keeping it brief and relevant.

Talking with God should be very natural and the children need to realise this. Explain that we say 'Amen' as a means of saying we agree. We don't have to close our eyes and put our hands together!

For more information on praying with children, check out *Top Tips on Prompting prayer*
SU, 978 1 84427 322 5
£2.99

Helping children to respond
Much of the material you will cover in *Rocky's Plaice* may prompt children to want to be friends with Jesus for themselves. Be ready to help them, but make sure that you stay within your church's child protection policy when praying with children.

- They rarely need long explanations, just simple answers to questions.
- Talk to them in a place where you can be seen by others.
- Never put pressure on children to respond in a particular way, just help them take one step closer to Jesus when they are ready. We don't want them to respond just to please us!
- Remember, for many children there are a number of commitments as their understanding grows.
- Many children just need a bit of help to say what they want to say to God. Here is a suggested prayer they could use to make a commitment to Jesus:

> Jesus, I want to be your friend.
> Thank you that you love me.
> Thank you for living in the world and dying on a cross for me.
> I'm sorry for all the wrong things I have done.
> Please forgive me and let me be your friend.
> Please let the Holy Spirit help me be like you.
>
> Amen.

- Reassure them that God hears us when we talk with him and has promised to forgive us and help us to be his friends. Children need help to stick with Jesus, especially if their parents don't believe.
- Assure them that God wants to hear whatever they say. Give them some prayer ideas.
- Encourage them to keep coming to Christian activities, not necessarily on Sundays – their church might have to be the midweek club or a school lunch-time club.
- Reading the Bible will be easier with something like *Snapshots* – but you need to support them if they are to keep it up.
- Keep praying and maintain your relationship with them wherever possible.

Friends with Jesus (for 5 to 7s), *Me+Jesus* (for 8s and 9s) and *Jesus=friendship forever* will help to explain what it means to follow Jesus. Details are on the inside front cover.

Equally, in the context of *Rocky's Plaice*, children may want to pray for God to fill them with the Holy Spirit, just as he filled the first disciples. When this occurs, really encourage the children. Ask them to explain what they understand and why they would like to pray. Pray a short simple prayer with faith. Encourage the children to pray themselves. When you have prayed, encourage the children that God has heard their prayer and that he will fulfil his promise. Check with them how they are feeling and if they have any questions.

For more information on helping children respond, see *Top Tips on Helping a child respond to Jesus*
SU, 978 1 84427 387 4
£2.99

Reading the Bible with children
At *Rocky's Plaice* we want children to understand that the Bible is God's Word for them today. It is important that the times when you read the Bible together are enjoyable and make sense to them! Children are not simply reading the Bible to get answers to our questions. Instead, we want their curiosity raised so that they can expect to meet God as they read the Bible, not just now, but in the future.

Rocky's Menu is there to help you read the relevant part of the Bible at the club. Make sure that you have a child-friendly version of the Bible with you which doesn't look tatty. (The CEV is the version used in *Rocky's Menu*) If you copy out the relevant verses onto paper or acetate, ensure that the children see that it is from the Bible.

Ask the team to think about how they read the Bible. How do they approach the book? Is it a pleasure or a chore? Get some feedback on people's attitude to the Bible, without being negative or judgemental. Comment that children will pick up on our attitudes to the Bible, and make their own opinions based on what they see us doing. Challenge the team to examine their own attitudes without making them feel unworthy!

Look at these tips together and discuss how you can apply them to your Bible exploration at *Rocky's Plaice*.

- Break a Bible passage into smaller chunks and go over it a little at a time.
- Think of ways to engage the children's thoughts as the verses are read. Help them listen. Suggestions for this have been given each day.
- Ask only a confident child to read out loud.
- Remember that many children find reading difficult, because of their age and/or educational ability. This does not stop them listening or using their imaginations to enter the Bible.
- This might be a child's first experience of Bible reading. Make it a positive one!
- You will need to explain about chapters and verses. Use page numbers where possible.
- Be prepared to recommend a Bible reading guide to follow up *Rocky's Plaice*.

Working with special needs

During *Rocky's Plaice* you will face a number of challenges. Being prepared to take care of children with special needs can be a tremendous blessing to both the children and their parent. Here are a few guidelines for working with children with special needs.

- Value every child as an individual. Before the start, find out as much as possible about them – their likes and dislikes, strengths and limitations. Then you will know how best to include them and make them feel safe.
- Prepare each session with a range of abilities in mind. Think carefully about working with abstract ideas. These may be misunderstood and taken literally! Have a range of craft ideas. Check that you do not give a child with learning difficulties a task that is appropriate for their reading age but inappropriate for their actual age. In other words, make sure that pictures and other aids are age-appropriate.
- Give all children opportunities to join in activities. Some children with special needs may have distinctive areas of interest or talents that you can encourage. As far as possible, keep children with

disabilities with their own peer group.

- If you have a child with hearing difficulties, make sure they sit near the front and that they can see the speaker's face clearly (not lit from behind). If a loop system is available, check that it is working for the child. Discussion in small groups can be hard for deaf children. Try to reduce background noise.
- Pay attention to any medical needs noted on the registration form, particularly any medication they take. Keep a record of any medication given, initialled by the first-aider and another team member.
- Designate leaders to work one-to-one with children with challenging behaviour. Where appropriate, set up a buddy system so that they work closely with a peer.
- Expect good behaviour from all children, but be tolerant of unusual behaviour. For example, some children need to fiddle with something in their hands.
- Ensure that all the children know what is planned for the day. Give the children a five-minute warning when an activity is about to finish. Some children need to finish one activity before they can concentrate on another.

Top tips on Welcoming special children
SU, 978 1 84427 126 9
£2.99

Helping children with special needs to know God is challenging, but deeply rewarding. Find out what the Bible has to say on the subject and explore the implications of the Disability Discrimination Act for your church. Be encouraged and inspired with stories from group leaders and parents, and be equipped with lots of practical ideas for welcoming special children in your church and children's group.

Working with children from other faith backgrounds

- We will not criticise, ridicule or belittle other religions.
- We will not tell the children what their faith says, nor define it by what some of its adherents do.
- We will not ask the children to say, sing or pray things that they do not believe, understand or that compromises their own faith.
- We will value and affirm the positive aspects of the children's culture.
- We will use music, artwork and methods that

are culturally appropriate. For example, Asian Christian music, pictures of people from a variety of backgrounds, single sex activities where deemed appropriate.

- We will be open and honest in our presentation of the Christian faith.
- We will be open and honest about the aims and content of our work with teachers, families, carers and other adults involved in their lives.
- We will seek to build long-term friendships that are genuine and not dependent on conversion.
- Talking of conversion with children of other faiths in isolation from their families is inappropriate.
- We are committed to the long-term nature of the work, for the children now and the impact this could have on future generations.
- Where children show a genuine interest in the Christian faith we will discuss how they can be a follower of Jesus and obey their parents, whilst being open and honest about the consequences.
- We will never suggest that the children keep things secret from their families or carers.

Top Tips on Welcoming children of other faiths

SU, 978 1 84427 250 1
£2.99
What does the Bible say about those of other faiths and how we should live out our faith amongst them? What can your church do? Here's a readable and practical guide which will inspire and equip you to build relationships with children and their families. It's packed with practical, fun ideas that will strengthen or even kick-start your ministry with those of other faiths.

SESSION 2
THE ROCKY'S PLAICE PROGRAMME

Use this session to go through some of the practical aspects of the club and to focus the team's minds on spiritual preparation for the club.

Welcome

Again, make sure you give the team a big welcome, ensuring refreshments are freely available, with the Rocky's Plaice theme song playing in the background as people arrive.

'God did it' – A Holy Spirit overview

During the week of Rocky's Plaice, the children and team will be introduced to some of the key stories from the life of the early church. One of the catchphrases used in the holiday club is, 'God did

it'. The story of the early church is very much God's story – Peter may be leader of the church, but God is the director. Set menu 2 tells the story of the Day of Pentecost when the Holy Spirit first came on the disciples. In fact, God the Holy Spirit is powerfully in action all the way through the book of Acts. Note: We are aware that different churches will handle the work of the Holy Spirit in different ways so you may want to adapt Rocky's Plaice to your own church's stance and practice in this area.

This Bible study is aimed at helping us remember and understand who the Holy Spirit is and what the key things are that he does in the lives of Christians today.

Challenge the group to discover some of the names for God the Holy Spirit in the Bible by giving them these references:
- Matthew 3:16 (the Spirit of God)
- Romans 8:9 (the Spirit of Christ)
- John 16:13 (the Spirit of Truth)
- John 14:26 (Counsellor/Helper)

Encourage the team that God is Spirit (John 14:26) and that God the Holy Spirit is God, just as the Father and Son are God. He is to be worshipped, sought after, loved and adored! He is God who lives in us. He is active!

Split into groups or pairs and give everyone one of the passages below. Ask them to see what they can learn from each passage about God the Holy Spirit and be ready to feed back what they have learnt.
- Acts 1:8; 2:38–40 (Power to live for Jesus – a promise for all believers)
- John 14:15–17 (Helper)
- John 16:13–15 (Leads into the truth and brings Jesus glory)
- Galatians 5:22–25 (Grows special fruit in us)
- 1 Corinthians 12:4–11 (Gives us special gifts)

After a few minutes ask the groups to feed back what they have learnt. The main points can be listed on some flip-chart paper.

Conclude this section by asking:
- Why is the Holy Spirit a great gift?
- What impact does the Holy Spirit have in our lives?
- What impact can the Holy Spirit have in the lives of children?

Note:

Praying for God the Holy Spirit to come and fill someone is a privilege and a responsibility. Being filled is a wonderful gift that should be treated with the utmost respect. The committed Christian should be constantly asking God to fill them up each day. Care should be taken when serving the children. God the Holy Spirit will be powerfully at work revealing the truth to the children. He loves them passionately and longs to live in them, producing the same fruit, gifting them, empowering them to live for him at home and at school. In the holiday club we will not be praying for God the Holy Spirit to fill each child – we will be praying that God will reveal himself to each one, leading them to a place of forgiveness and infilling. As we will see in the 'Praying with Children' section, care will be needed on how we communicate these things to the children.

Pray and thank God for his wonderful gift of the Holy Spirit. Pray together that God will fill you up individually and anoint you as a team for the task ahead.

Practicalities

Rocky's Plaice
Explain the overall themes of *Rocky's Plaice* (see page 6) and explain a little of the desire to show what it means to be one of God's people and part of the Church. Also, introduce the team to the Learn and remember verse (John 3:16), the *Rocky's Plaice* theme song, the Deep Fat Fryer, Captain Ketchup and the other recurring elements of the programme.

Take the team through a day's programme, making sure that everyone knows where all the different parts will take place and their responsibilities in each one.

The aims of Rocky's Plaice
Make sure everyone has a copy of the general aims of *Rocky's Plaice* (see page 6) and the specific aims for your club. Split into smaller groups to discuss these aims – can the groups identify any other aims? This will help you refine your aims and encourage your team to take ownership of them.

Legal requirements
Cover health and safety, risk assessments, fire procedures and basic child protection information – if your church has a coordinator for this, they should be able to help out at this point. Alternatively, contact CCPAS or visit their website: **www.ccpas.co.uk**

Prayer
Spend some time together as a team praying for each other, for *Rocky's Plaice* and for all the children who will come.

This can be done in many ways. It would be great to get the leaders of each Guest Group to pray together. You may wish to use some of the creative prayer ideas you will find in each day's session outlines.

Further training
Over the past three years, Scripture Union has produced training features to go alongside holiday club programmes. These would be ideal for further training, not only with your holiday club team, but with those who work with children throughout the year:

On the *Showstoppers!* DVD (SU, 978 1 84427 344 7), there is a training feature on communicating with children and telling your own story. On the *Champion's Challenge* DVD (SU, 978 1 84427 331 7), there is a training feature on expanding your church's ministry beyond a five-day holiday club. Many churches run midweek clubs, put on special holiday club events at other times of the year and hold other events to grow relationships created at holiday clubs. On the *Wastewatchers* DVD (SU, 978 1 84427 246 4), the training feature centres on making connections with the families of children you have contact with through holiday clubs.

SU also produces *Top Tips*, a series of books containing practical advice on a variety of subjects. *Top Tips on Growing faith with families* and *Top Tips on Reaching unchurched children* would be ideal training tools for team training.

Top Tips on Growing faith with families
SU, 978 1 84427 249 5
£2.99
What does the Bible say about families? What can your church do for families? Here's a readable and practical guide which will inspire and equip you to reach out to families in your community. It's packed with practical, fun ideas that will make a real difference to mums, dads, and children.

Top Tips on Reaching unchurched children
SU, 978 1 84427 127 6
£2.99
How do we talk about God to children who know next to nothing about him? Be inspired by some biblical principles on evangelism and find out how to build relationships through natural points of contact with children outside the church.

Fourth course Resource bank
In the larder

Songs

ROCKY'S PLAICE THEME SONG

The theme song provides a soundtrack to your club, helps develop an identity to your club and is fun to sing! Sheet music and words are on pages 48–49, the song itself is available on the *Rocky's Plaice* DVD. Suggested actions for the song are:

Verse 1

All lines start with gentle rock motion as if playing air guitar and rocking away!
Line 1: Rock, then make the shape of a house using hands in time to the beat.
Line 2: Rise up from low position with hands 'measuring the levels'.
Line 3: Punch chest over heart with right fist.

Verse 2

All lines start with gentle rock motion as if playing air guitar and rocking away!
Line 1: Give yourself a big hug.
Line 2: Shout out 'Tell the world!' with hands cupped over mouth.
Line 3: Double thumbs up!

Chorus

Line 1: Give other people high fives.
Line 2: Shake hands with as many people as possible.
Line 3: Fancy guitar poses, before beginning to properly 'air guitar' rock on the word rock.
Line 4: Serious air guitar rocking.

Outro

Line 1: In guitar pose, turn 90 degrees anticlockwise on first 'rocky',
Line 2: Turn another 90 degrees anticlockwise on first 'rocky'
Line 3: Turn another 90 degrees anticlockwise on first 'rocky'
Line 4: Turn back to front for 'rock the world…'!

LEARN AND REMEMBER VERSE SONG

The Learn and remember verse for the week is John 3:16. This is probably the best known Bible verse ever, and for good reason! It tells us why God sent Jesus in the first place, and gives us a great promise for those who believe in him! It is worth explaining the following:

■ Believing is not just something we think, but something that affects our whole lives. So Jesus' promise is for those who by word and deed show they are following!
■ The recorded version uses the words 'will never die'. This does not mean that our bodies will never die; it is referring to our spirits. Our spirits go and live with Jesus even when our bodies die.

There is a song to help children learn the verse; you can find the sheet music and words for it on pages 50-57. There is a recording on the the *Rocky's Plaice* DVD. There is an alternative song on the album *Amazing* by Dave Godfrey, which includes another 14 tracks you might find useful during the club.

There are some simple actions to help remember the verse. (Children learn better if they are active, rather than passive!) If you decide to use the song, these can become the actions to the song too!

God loved you, *(Point both index fingers to someone else)*
God loved me, *(Point thumbs to yourself)*
God loved the world so much! *(Draw big circular shape with hands to represent the world)*
God loved you, *(as above)*
God loved me, *(as above)*

God loved the world so much that he sent his Son *(Draw big circular shape with hands to reprenet the world, then go to a big double thumbs up, looking up.)*

Now everyone who believes in him, *(march around on the spot anti-clockwise)*
Will never die, *(continue marching, then freeze on 'die')*
And everyone who believes in him, *(march around on the spot clockwise)*
Will live for ever more! *(Criss-cross with legs)*

Verse 16, John chapter 3, *(Hold up six, then ten, then three fingers in time)*
We can live for eternity! *(Do the twist!)*

Games

Use a selection of these games during Ice cream crazy every day.

FISH FLAPPING

What you need
- Newspapers
- Fish shapes cut out of newspaper

What you do
Line the Guest Groups up behind the start line. In turn, the children have to bash their newspaper on the floor behind a fish to make it move to the end of the room. They should then run back and give the newspaper and fish to the next child, and so on until the whole Group has finished. The first group to finish is the winner.

FISH AND CHIP CHEF'S HAT CHALLENGE

What you need
- Large pile of newspapers or a roll of newsprint (end rolls are available from printers for a small charge or for free)
- Sticky tape, scissors and felt-tip pens per Guest Group

What you do
Show an example of a chef's hat to the children and explain how to make one (this can be as elaborate or as simple as you like). Working in Guest Groups, the children should make chef's hats and decorate them as they like. Allow ten minutes for the children to do this and then show off the designs to each other and maybe the whole holiday club.

PICKLED ONION PARACHUTE FOOTBALL

What you need
- Parachute
- Soft ball
- Whistle (for keeping control!)

What you do
Split the children into two teams – name them Fish and Chips. They then face each other over the parachute. Two team leaders play the role of referee and assistant referee and stand opposite each other and between the teams. A soft ball (designated a pickled onion) is thrown onto the parachute. A goal is scored when the pickled onion flies off the parachute over the side of the opposing team. A goal is also conceded if the children handle the pickled onion, although they are allowed to head the onion.

For more parachute games, see page 22 to 25 of *Ultimate Games* (SU, 978 1 84427 365 2, £9.99).

MUSTARD ATTACK!

What you need
- Large hoops
- Stickers
- Music and whistle

What you do
Place a number of hoops around the room and nominate a small number of leaders or children as Mustard Merchants. Play the music and encourage the children to dance to the music (maybe gaining extra boogie points for outrageous dancing!), but they should keep out of the hoops. After a while, shout 'Mustard attack!' The children then have to run into the safety of the nearest hoop. If the Mustard Merchants are able to stick a sticker on a child before they enter the safety of the hoop, they are out and have to sit out the next round in the Mustard Purification Station (an area to the side of the playing area). Gradually the number of children playing is reduced until you have some winners who could be rewarded with a giant 'wnner' sticker. If you have different colour hoops you can make an extra shout to warn that some are not safe, eg 'Mustard attack – red hoops are infected.' This adds extra panic and fun to the game. It is worth talking through with the children the need to be thoughtful and safe as they play.

IN THE CHIPPER

What you need
- A 'chipper' (a goal made up of two cones)
- Several wooden spoons
- Potatoes

What you do
Line the Guest Groups up behind the start line. Each group is given a chipper to aim for and two wooden spoons. In pairs, the children have to guide a potato placed on the floor behind the start line into the chipper (set several metres away) using only the wooden spoons. As soon as the potato is in the chipper the wooden spoons are given to the next group members. The winning group have the most potatoes in the chipper by the end of the allotted time.

MEAL MADNESS

What you need
- Buckets
- Plastic or paper plates
- Pictures of five meals, laminated and cut up into four pieces

What you do
Line the Guest Groups up in lines behind the start line. Each group is given a bucket, set a distance away from the start line; in it are the pieces of the cut-up meals. Each group also has five plates behind the start line. The children take it in turns to run to the bucket, rescue one piece of a meal and bring it back to their group. As more pieces are collected, the group has to match the meal pieces with each other to create five complete meals. The first group to finish the challenge is the winner.

(This game was adapted from an idea by YoYo Trust, York.)

For more games of all kinds, check out
Ultimate Games
SU, 978 1 84427 365 2
£9.99

Craft

Use a selection of these craft ideas during Ice cream crazy every day.

HAMA BEAD COASTERS

What you need
- Hama beads and boards (available from toy and craft shops)
- Iron (and adult to use it) and ironing paper

What you do
Set out Hama boards and beads for the children to choose from. You might like to provide some food designs for the children to follow, or encourage them to come up with their own ideas. When they have finished their coasters, they should take them very carefully to the leader responsible for ironing the beads together. They can be taken home at the end of the morning, or displayed at *Rocky's Plaice* and taken home at the end of the week.

DORCAS PRAYER BLANKETS/ BANNERS

What you need
- Large base sheet
- Squares of material (about 15 cm by 15 cm)
- Fabric pens or other decorative materials
- Sewing machine (and adult to use it)

What you do
Give each child a square of material and encourage them to decorate it. They can use scenes from the stories they hear from Peter, write encouraging messages or decorate the key word for the day. When the children have finished, a leader should gather the squares together and sew them onto the base sheet (this could be done outside the club time). You will have created a beautiful hope-filled blanket or banner that can be displayed at the club, hung in the church for the family service, given away or auctioned for charity.

ROCKY'S PLAICE PLACE MATS

What you need
- A4 sheets of paper
- Laminator (and adult to use it)
- Felt-tip pens or other art materials

What you do
Give each child a sheet of A4 paper and encourage them to create their own *Rocky's Plaice* picture. If you wish you could use the designs on the *Rocky's Plaice* website. When these have been completed they can be laminated as place mats that the children can then take home.

ROCKY'S PLAICE BUNTING

What you need
- Coloured paper or fabric, cut into triangles
- String
- Staplers or sticky tape
- Felt-tip pens

What you do
Give out the triangles of paper or fabric and encourage the children to draw a picture, write a key word or decorate them however they wish. Staple or stick the finished triangles to a long piece of string to create bunting. Use the bunting to decorate the Guest Group areas or the whole of *Rocky's Plaice*!

POTATO PRINTS

What you need
- Large sheets of paper
- Potatoes
- Paint
- Knife (adult use only)

What you do
Before the session, cut the potatoes in half and cut a variety of designs into the potato halves. Give these potato halves to the children and encourage them to make pictures by using the potatoes to print shapes with paint. When the pictures are dry, they can be taken home or displayed in Guest Group areas.

FISH COOKIES

What you need
- Simple biscuit mixture
- Rolling pins
- Biscuit cutters (fish-shaped if possible)
- Baking facilities (and adult to use them)
- Decorations (sultanas, Smarties, chocolate chips etc)
- Food bags or food wrap

What you do
After ensuring the children have clean hands, share out the biscuit dough and show the children how to roll it out and cut out shapes. After they have cut out their biscuits and decorated them as they wish, bake them as the children complete the rest of the morning's activities ready to be taken home at the end of the day.

Alternatively, you could provide pre-cooked biscuits and decorate these with icing as well as sultanas, chocolate drops etc.

As always when working with food, ensure that you check if any children have allergies and take appropriate steps to keep them safe.

For more craft ideas, see
Ultimate Craft
SU, 978 1 84427 364 5
£12.99

Drama

THE ADVENTURES OF SALT AND VINEGAR

Setting

The kitchen of *Rocky's Plaice* restaurant

Cast

- **Mr Tagliatelle**: The head chef at *Rocky's Plaice* and mentor to Salt and Vinegar. Mr Tagliatelle could speak with an Italian accent.
- **Salt**: Trainee chef at *Rocky's Plaice*. The more intelligent of the two trainee chefs.
- **Vinegar**: Trainee chef at *Rocky's Plaice*. Not quite as bright as Salt.
- **Charlie Chutney**: The TV star who eventually hires Salt and Vinegar in **Set menu 5**.
- **Customer**: An angry offstage voice in **Set menu 5**.

Salt, Vinegar and Chutney could be played by either male or female actors.

Costumes

All except Chutney should be dressed up as chefs/cooks. From **Special menu A**, Salt and Vinegar should wear commercial paper chef hats, onto which their reward stickers can be stuck. Chutney should wear a suit and look very important!

Props

For the set, you'll need a table as a work surface. A few extra kitchen props could be added to make the stage area look like a kitchen. For all episodes, you'll need a set of stickers. Any extra props are listed with each sketch.

Introduction

As part of a Chef Training Scheme, Salt and Vinegar join the kitchen team at *Rocky's Plaice* at the beginning of the week. Each day they gain valuable experience by completing a set of tasks given to them by Mr Tagliatelle. Their aim each day is to win a Silver Star sticker. Five Silver Star stickers will qualify them for the Super Star Chef Award. Unfortunately Mr Tagliatelle, their mentor, is always very busy, leaving Salt and Vinegar to fend for themselves in their quest for the top award. This leads to quite a few disasters, a lot of mess, silliness and fun! The story contains a twist in **Set menu 5**.

The sketches are slapstick and funny in style and should be played with lots of movement, silliness and speed. The sketches themselves are loosely connected to the theme for the day, but they are not trying to make any serious teaching points!

Set menus 1 to 5 stand alone. **Special menu A** and **Special menu B** have been written for the all-age services that might precede and follow *Rocky's Plaice*. They are not essential but will help the wider church to get a feel of what is going on!

Salt and Vinegar's song

In each of the main five episodes, Salt and Vinegar interact with the children with their theme song. It is very simple and goes to the tune of 'Head, shoulders, knees and toes'.

> Salt, Salt and Vinegar, Vinegar,
> Salt, Salt and Vinegar, Vinegar.
> We're the trainee chefs down in *Rocky's Plaice*!
> Salt, Salt and Vinegar, Vinegar.
>
> Salt, Salt and Vinegar, Vinegar,
> Salt, Salt and Vinegar, Vinegar.
> We're the trainee chefs who make a lot of mess!
> Salt, Salt and Vinegar, Vinegar.

Ideally a set of simple actions or a simple dance could be made up to accompany the song. You could use the actions for 'Head, shoulders, knees and toes'.

Mr Tagliatelle's names

In **Set menu 1**, Salt and Vinegar set the children the challenge of making up some rhyming names for Mr Tagliatelle, eg Mr Wobbly-belly. The children could either put them in the Deep Fat Fryer's chip pan or in a special bin, marked 'Salt and Vinegar'.

Salt and Vinegar should choose the names to read out before the sketches, even if they are pretending to go to the bin to get them directly out of the bin. This will enable them to check they can read the suggestions and that they have an appropriate number for that day's sketch.

The hidden camera

Salt and Vinegar discover in **Set menu 5** that all their kitchen disasters have been caught on camera. The camera needs to be visible from the beginning of the holiday club as it is referred to in each sketch. A small 10 cm cardboard box or piece of wood could be painted yellow and a 3 cm diameter black circle could be added as a camera lens.

Photographs

In **Special menu B**, Salt and Vinegar relive some of their best moments from the week. It would be helpful for those who have not been at *Rocky's Plaice*, if some photographs could be taken during **Set menus 1 to 5** of the moments mentioned in **Special menu B**, so they can then be shown on the screen.

SPECIAL MENU A

Props

- Card and other hat-making equipment
- A chef's hat that has already been created and decorated
- Fast background music

Script

T: *(Coming on and addressing audience.)* Welcome to my kitchen. My name is Tagliatelle. I am head chef here at *Rocky's Plaice*. Today, as part of the brand new Chef Training Scheme I am pleased to welcome two new trainee chefs. Please put your hands together for Salt and Vinegar! *(Salt and Vinegar appear on stage a bit sheepish, dressed as chefs except they are not wearing hats.)* This is Salt *(Puts arm around Salt's shoulders.)* and this is Vinegar. *(Puts arm around Vinegar's shoulders.)* Salt and Vinegar, tell all the guests something about yourselves!

S: Hi, my name is Salt, I'm *[age]* years old. I have a pet gerbil called Clarence. I really like playing football and watching *Doctor Who* defeat the Daleks!

V: Hi, my name is Vinegar, I'm *[age]* years old. I like sitting down in front of the telly with Bananas on my lap. Sometimes I even walk around with Bananas on my head. Sometimes I take Bananas for a walk! I even like talking to Bananas.

T: Are you crazy?

V: No, I just love my pet frog, he's called Bananas!

T: Oh… very good – you are both really welcome here at *Rocky's Plaice*. Your challenge this week is to become Super Star Chefs. To qualify as a Super Star Chef, you need to win five Silver Star Stickers for acts of cooking brilliance. I will be awarding the stickers and I am confident you two young chefs will be perfect and brilliant! *(S and V look at each other and nod!)* Now there is one thing that is missing.

S: That's probably Vinegar's brain!

V: Which one?

T: You two need to make yourselves chef's hats! Each day I am going to give you a different challenge to help you become Super Star Chefs – today it is to make a chef's hat! Here is a table; here are some pieces of equipment. You have two minutes to complete the task! *(Mr Tagliatelle exits, running.)*

S: OK, here we go.

Fast music is played in the background as Salt makes a ridiculous hat to go on Vinegar's head. Some ad-libbing can happen in this section. It takes the full two minutes to complete Vinegar's hat.

T: *(Coming back on.)* Ten seconds left!

V: How do I look?

S: Fantastic… and maybe a bit ridiculous!

V: Where's your hat then?

S: Er… oh dear… *(Pulling out a hidden, completed hat.)* Oh yes, here's one I made earlier!

T: Time's up! Salt – that is a most impressive hat! Vinegar – that is also a very impressive hat, if a little strange! I award you… *(He pauses.)* half a sticker each!

S and V: Thank you sir!

T: Tomorrow I want perfection!

S: Er Mr T, we'd like to say thank you for having us this week – we are hoping to learn loads from you and to do a really good job!

V: We are salt and vinegar and we think that you, Mr My-feet-are-smelly, are the greatest, and we think, this week, we can learn so much from you! You are like the topping on our pizza, the icing on our cake, the tomato ketchup on our cornflakes.

T: The tomato ketchup on your cornflakes?

V: Em, yes, the tomato ketchup on our cornflakes!

T: I love tomato ketchup on everything. Sounds wonderful! Anyway, the real action begins tomorrow. I need you both back here for some expert lessons from yours truly – Mr Tagliatelle! Goodbye everyone!

Mr T leaves. S and V wander off slowly behind him chatting.

V: I thought his name was Mr My-feet-are-smelly!

S: Shh – he'll hear you!

S and V: *(To audience.)* See ya!

They exit.

SET MENU 1

THE FISH-BATTERING CHALLENGE

Props

- Note from Mr Tagliatelle
- Three buckets: one containing confetti, one containing water and one containing a cardboard or plastic fish.
- Wooden spoon
- Feather duster
- Rounders bat
- Black 'paint'
- Big cardboard box marked as deep fat fryer (one side needs to be open to put in extra props)
- Bowl with flour already in it
- Super Soaker water gun full of water
- Vinegar's bag containing: a pair of trainers, a Mars Bar and a pet frog

Script

S: Good morning Vinegar.

V: Morning Salt.

S: Wahey – it's our first real day as trainee chefs here at *Rocky's Plaice* – the coolest fish and chip restaurant in town!

V: We're hoping to have a great week learning from Mr Watch-er-the-telly – the head chef!

S: I'm not sure Mr Watch-er-the-telly is his real name.

V: It's something like that – maybe it's Mr There's-a-rumble-in-my-belly!

S: No, his real name is Mr Tagliatelle!

V: Oh yes! Psst – have you spotted the guests? *(Points to the children.)*

S: Wow, welcome everyone to *Rocky's Plaice*. My name is Salt.

V: And my name is Vinegar, and we're new here, like you – and we're learning how to cook.

S: In fact we're training to be Super Star Chefs.

V: To become Super Star Chefs, we need to win five Silver Star Stickers each for acts of cooking brilliance. We've already won half a sticker each *(Shows sticker on hat.)* for making some chefs hats. We need four and a half more stickers before the end of the week to be… *(Pauses, then shouts.)* Super Star Chefs!

S: The stickers are awarded by the head chef here at *Rocky's Plaice*.

V: *(To S.)* Did Mr Wobbly-belly say he'd meet us here for our first lesson?

S: The head chef's name is Mr Tagliatelle, and he must be running late!

V: Maybe we should introduce the guests here to the song we just made up while we're waiting!

S: What song?

V: You know…

S and V introduce and perform the Salt and Vinegar song. Then they encourage the children to join in.

S: That was great!

V: Mr Wobbly-belly still hasn't turned up! *(Points to the hidden camera.)* Hey, what's that yellow box on the wall?

S: *(Seeing note on floor.)* Oh look, there are some instructions here on the floor. *(Picks it up and reads it.)* It says, 'I'm sorry I'm not able to join you this morning; I've had to go and get some extra potatoes. Please could you batter the fish for me?' Where's the fish?

V: I'll look in these buckets. *(Picks up first bucket and pours confetti on himself.)* It's not in here! *(Picks up second bucket and pours water on himself.)* It's not in here either! *(Picks up third bucket and just before he tips it up, spots the fish.)* It's in here!

S: Great!

V: *(Putting bucket on the table.)* What did he want us to do with the fish?

S: He says he wants us to batter the fish!

V: Are you sure he wants us to batter the fish?

S: Yep – but how do you batter a fish?

V: I know – Salt, you hold the fish by the tail and I'll batter it! *(Picks up a wooden spoon and hits it several times.)*

S: My turn. *(Repeats the action with roles reversed.)*

V: There must be a better way of battering this fish!

S: We could put it on the table and hit it! *(Does so.)*

V: We could batter it with a feather duster… *(Picks up feather duster and tries it.)* But you don't feel like you're battering it when you hit it with a feather duster!

S: How about using a rounders bat! *(Picks up bat and takes a swing.)*

V: Hold on – maybe we've got it wrong. Real bats are black aren't they? If we need to batter it, all we need to do is paint it black!

S: OK I've got some black paint – let's start painting! *(Paints the fish.)*

V: Maybe if we batter the black battered fish with the bat it will be truly battered!

S picks up fish as if bowling as a cricketer and V picks up rounders bat to batter the fish as if batting as a cricketer. Both freeze as Mr T walks in before the ball has been bowled!

T: *(Has not seen what S and V are doing.)* Right my lovely trainee chefs. You should have the flour and water mixed together by now, creating a beautiful batter for battering my delicious fish! We can then put the battered fish in this lovely deep fat fryer! *(Turns to S and V.)*

S: Err…

V: Err…

T: Oh my goodness, what are you doing?

V: Battering this black battered fish with a rounders bat!

T: You two are hopeless! *(Checks watch.)* I cannot stop though! Mix this flour *(Puts bowl of flour on table.)* with some water to make the batter, dip the fish in the batter and pop it in this deep fat fryer! *(He exits.)*

S: *(Calling after Mr T.)* Yes Mr Wobbly-jelly!

V: *(Calling after Mr T.)* Sorry Mr Give-the-ball-some-welly!

S: He's gone. Mr Give-the-ball-some-welly – that's a great name!

V: Wouldn't it be great if the children came up with some really cool new names for Mr Tagliatelle? The names have to rhyme of course, like 'Wobbly-belly', 'I'm-on-the-telly'.

S: Great idea! Children, can you put any of your suggestions in our Salt and Vinegar bin – we'll then use some of your made up names in the sketches!

V: Back to our battering – what do we need to do?

S: He said mix this flour with water to make some batter. I've got the flour – we need water!

V: I know! *(Goes to his bag and rescues his Super Soaker.)* Hold still… *(Wets S and the children a bit.)*

S: He said dip the fish in the batter, then bung them in the deep fat fryer!

V: We can't use the fish – it's got paint on it!

S: Maybe we should batter something else then!

V: I've got some other things in my bag!

S: We could batter your trainers! *(Puts trainers in the deep fat fryer.)*

V: We could batter a Mars Bar! *(Takes a bite, then puts Mars Bar in the deep fat fryer.)*

S: We could batter Bananas! *(Gets pet frog out of bag.)*

V: You can't batter Bananas – my poor pet frog! *(Talks to the frog.)* Oh he didn't mean it! My poor little fruitcake!

T: *(Entering.)* Right then you two… *(Salt and Vinegar freeze.)* Oh what a mess! How's the fish? What? You're deep fat frying training shoes and Mars Bars? Oh my goodness! What hope is there for these two? *(S and V cringe but remain frozen. T turns to audience.)* Wonderful guests, I am truly sorry about the mess. The trainee chefs are new, and I couldn't help them do the battering today. This won't happen again – I am full of hope! *(To S and V.)* Salt and Vinegar, I want you in my office in one minute! *(Exits grumbling.)*

S: Oopsy.

V: Oopsy-doopsy.

S: I'm not sure we're going to win any stickers after today's cooking!

V: It was fun though.

S: We have learnt something though, haven't we!

V: We learnt that you don't need a wooden spoon, a feather duster, a rounders bat or black paint to batter a fish!

S: You just need flour and water, and a deep fat fryer!

V: I'm sure we're going to learn loads this week!

S: It's time to go. Don't forget those other names for Mr Wobbly-jelly!

V: Bye everyone!

S: Bye – I hope tomorrow's as much fun!

Both exit.

SET MENU 2

THE ULTIMATE CELEBRATION COMBINATION PIE CHALLENGE

Props

- Note from Mr Tagliatelle
- Bag containing fish fingers, custard, ice cream, toy gerbil, plastic frog, gravy, mushroom and toothpaste
- Four small pie bases/foil dishes
- Teaspoons for tasting
- Bag containing pie base, squirty cream and strawberries
- Paper plates
- Knife
- Fast music
- Recipe card

Script

S: Good morning Vinegar!

V: Good morning Salt!

S and **V**: (To audience.) Good morning everyone!

S: I can feel a song coming on!

V: Come on everyone, stand up and join in!

Everyone sings the Salt and Vinegar song.

S: Great stuff.

V: How many stickers have we got so far then?

S: Half each!

V: We had half each at the beginning of yesterday.

S: Well, we didn't exactly show any cooking brilliance with our fish battering did we?

V: Our ears got a bit of a battering from Mr My-feet-are-so-smelly.

S: Hey, that's a great name – I've got a few names here from some of the children. (*Reads out some of the names suggested by the children and the names of the children who have made them up.*)

V: Great names! But Mr I-can-buy-cheese-in-the-deli is nowhere to be seen!

S: Oh look, he's left another note!

V: What does it say?

S: It says, 'Sorry Salt and Vinegar, I may be a bit late, but I should be back in a bit. Here is today's challenge. I need you to make some ultimate celebration combination pies. Please use the ingredients provided! PS After the fish disaster yesterday, I want perfection!'

V: Making pies sounds fun. Where's the bag of ingredients?

S: Must be this bag over here! (*Picks up bag containing fish fingers, custard, toy gerbil, cream, plastic frog, gravy, mushroom and toothpaste.*)

V: Good. Where are the pie bases to put them in?

S: Must be these pie bases over here! (*Picks them up and puts on table.*)

V: Let's make those pies!

Fast music plays in the background. S and V start to make their pies with some accidental lathering each other, silly dancing, throwing utensils to each other etc. At the end of about two minutes music, Mr T comes in and S and V freeze.

T: (*Not looking at S and V.*) Right my lovely trainee chefs. You have had enough time to put the lovely ingredients into the beautiful pastry to make the most delicious pies! (*Turns to S and V.*) Oh my goodness, what are you doing?

S: Err…

V: Err…

S: Making some ultimately beautiful pie combinations.

V: Mr My-brothers-a-he, would you like to try some of our combinations?

T: Have you made some new combinations?

S: Yes I think we might have – try this one! (*Mr T tries pie one.*)

T: Not bad – what is it?

V: Fish fingers and custard.

T: (*Pulling a face.*) Interesting – let me try the next combination. (*Tries pie two.*)

S: It's a personal favourite of mine: gerbil and ice cream pie!

T: (*Spluttering.*) Gerbil and ice cream pie? A very interesting combination!

V: How about trying combination three, chef?

T: (*Tasting it.*) Mmmm – very nice, what's this?

S: Banana and gravy pie!

T: (*Starting to cough.*) Yuck!

V: Bananas! Oh poor Bananas, my poor pet frog! (*Rescues pet frog, then trys to comfort it.*) He didn't mean it… no he didn't mean it!

S: We've got one more – combination four.

T: Oh I like the smell … let me taste … vegetarian with a hint of mint! Oh, this is delicious, totally marvellous. Fantastic… an act of cooking brilliance. A taste and combination so profound that I have to immediately give you both a Silver Sticker!

V: Wahey!

T: Such a marvellous combination… vegetarian with a hint of mint, wouldn't you say?

S: Very close – it's actually mushroom and toothpaste.

T: (*Gagging.*) Eurgh!

V: That combination is my favourite!

S: Me too!

T: Why didn't you use the recipe card?

S: The recipe card?

V: What recipe card?

T: This one. (*Finds it on the floor.*) 'How to make ultimate celebration combination pies.' (*Hands card to S* *and V.)*

S: We must have got the wrong bag of ingredients.

V: It doesn't have custard in it.

S: It doesn't have gerbil in it.

V: It doesn't have toothpaste in it.

S: It doesn't even have Bananas in it.

V: Oh what a relief! *(Talks to pet frog like to a baby.)* You're safe my little beautiful darling froggy woggy!

T: No it does not – it has the most delicious, beautiful, tender strawberries, with delicious cream!

From another bag on the floor, he takes out a pie base, strawberries and cream and makes a pie.

S: Oh.

V: Oh.

T: It doesn't take long to make the ultimate celebration combination pie! Got to go… *(Walks off eating the pie.)*

S: So, Vinegar, my old buddy.

V: Yes, Salt, me old pal.

S: We somehow managed to earn a silver sticker each!

V: Amazing! Vegetarian with a hint of mint! Brilliant!

S: We also learnt something very important.

V: We've learnt – it's the filling that counts.

S: Indeed we did – it's really important for our pies to be filled with the right filling!

V: Have you noticed we've made a bit of a mess again?

S: It was fun though.

V: I actually quite fancy the gerbil and ice cream pie!

S: I quite fancy a Bananas pie – where's your frog?

V: Arrrrgggghhhh! *(Runs off, talking to the frog.)* I'll protect you froggy woggy!

S: Bye everyone… see you tomorrow!

As he walks off, S notices the camera, studies it for a moment then continues off.

S: *(Just before exiting.)* Bye!

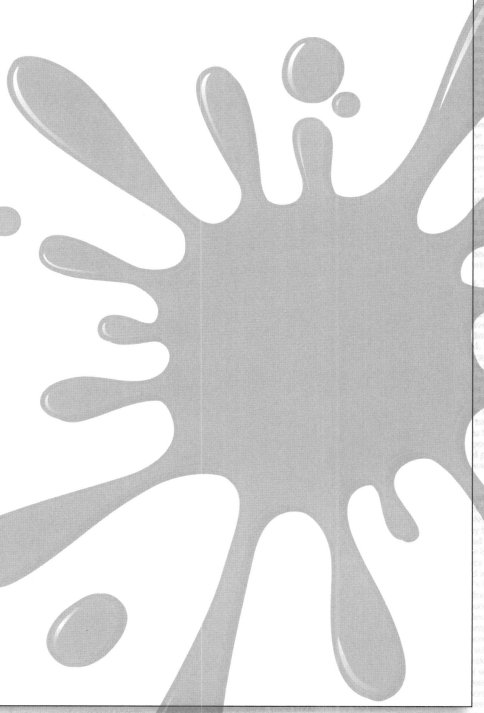

SET MENU 3

THE CELEBRATION CAKE CHALLENGE

Props

- Recipe card
- Plastic frog
- Fake cake ingredients: rope for bull, plastic flower
- Bowl, wooden spoon
- Real cake ingredients: butter, milk, flour, sugar
- Pretend oven
- Cake that is undecorated
- Cream
- Six eggs in a box – three raw and three hard-boiled, with note
- Towel
- Cake tin
- TV 'muzak'
- Table cloth

Script

S: *(Singing.)* Oh what a glorious morning…

V: *(Singing.)* Oh what a beautiful day…

S: *(Singing.)* We're gonna do some more cooking…

V: *(Singing.)* And nothing can get in the way!

S: Good morning everyone!

V: Look, we're the proud owners of one and half Silver Star stickers!

S: Yep, we only need three and a half more to be Super Star Chefs!

V: *(Going over to the hidden camera.)* I wonder what this is then?

S: What, that yellow thing?

V: Yeah, what do you think it is?

S: Maybe it's one of those special smoke sensors?

V: We'd better not burn our dishes today then.

S: Oh, forget about that. Let's check out what's in our bin today.

V: *(Getting names out of the bin.)* We've got some great names for Mr When-I've-had-a-bath-I'm-not-smelly. Here

– you have half and I'll have half.

They share out the names, but before they can read them, Mr T comes in. S and V stand to attention as though on parade.

T: Right then you two. Are you ready to do some cooking?

S: *(To Mr T.)* Yes Mr AAAAAA! *(Reads out a name from the bin.)*

V: *(To Mr T.)* Yes Mr BBBBB! *(Another name from the bin.)*

T: Salt and Vinegar, are you going to make any mistakes today?

S: *(To Mr T.)* No Mr CCCCC! *(Another name from the bin.)*

V: *(To Mr T.)* No Mr DDDDD! *(Another name from the bin.)*

T: Do you believe them, children?

Children: No!

T: *(To S and V.)* Are you ready for my challenge today?

S: *(To Mr T.)* Yes Mr EEEEE! *(Another name from the bin.)*

V: *(To Mr T.)* Yes Mr FFFFFF! *(Another name from the bin.)*

T: *(Moving around the back of S and V to stand between their shoulders.)* And your challenge today is to make a Celebration Cake to be shared amongst our lovely guests. Here is the recipe card! Good luck! *(Exits.)*

S: He's gone again!

V: I think he trusts us to do a good job for him today.

S: No mistakes.

V: Absolutely no mistakes!

S: What do we need? Ah, here it is according to the recipe card… I feel like saying this in a French accent… We need a bowl. *(Says this in French accent.)*

V goes off stage, picks up one end of a rope and pulls it onstage, as if pulling a giant bull.

V: I don't think the bull wants to come in!

S: No you banana – a bowl, not a bull – here's one! *(Gives a plastic bowl to V, who drops the rope. S then begins to wander around the stage, ignoring what V does.)*

S: We need flour.

V: Got it! *(V finds plastic flower and puts it on the bowl.)*

S: We need a yoke.

V: I've got a good yoke. *(To the children.)* Knock knock!

Children: Who's there?

V: Emma.

Children: Emma who?

V: Emma cracking you up!

S: No, we need an egg yoke.

V: Err, I thought that was one. *(To the children.)* Knock knock!

Children: Who's there?

V: Egg.

Children: Egg who?

V: Eggstremely cold milk is beautiful on cornflakes!

S: Milk.

V: Milk. *(Puts milk in bowl.)*

S: Butter.

V: Butter. *(Puts butter in bowl.)*

S: Sugar.

V: Sugar. *(Puts sugar in bowl.)*

S: *(Coming over to check bowl.)* What's this? *(Picks up flower.)*

V: You said flower!

S: Not that sort of flower – flour! Flour! Like this! *(Gives V the flour.)*

V: Sorry.

S: And where are the yokes?

V: I've already told two yokes!

S: We need eggs – like these – we need the yokes inside!

V: Oh look, this box has got a note on top of it. It says that three of these eggs are hard-boiled and three are raw.

S: We need the raw ones – we'll have to find out which ones are which!

V: OK I'll go first! *(Picks up hard-boiled egg and splats it on S's head.)* That one's hard-boiled!

S: My turn. *(Picks up raw egg and splats V.)* That's a raw one!

V: My turn. *(Picks up hard-boiled egg and splats it on S's head.)* That's another one hard-boiled!

S: My turn. *(Picks up raw egg and splats V.)* It's another raw one!

V: My turn... hold on… I'll let you take your turn next.

S: OK! *(Picks up raw egg and splats V.)* Oh dear it's another raw one! Ha ha!

V: This isn't fair!

S: Hold on, we need some of the egg for the cake! Hold your head over the bowl! *(Takes some of the egg off V's head and puts it in the bowl.)*

V: So have we got everything we need? *(Finds a towel to wipe his hair.)*

S: I think so. Let's pretend we're on TV. I'll be the chef and you can be my glamorous assistant. *(Turns to audience, gentle 'muzak' begins in background.)* Good morning viewers. My name is Salt and here is Vinegar, my glamorous assistant.

V: Hello! *(Takes towel off head to reveal hair in a real state!)*

S: Today we are making a cake! First you put the flour in the bowl – which it is. Then you mix in the butter, like this. Oops, we need to take the wrapper off. Please can you take the wrapper off for me, my glamorous assistant? The next step is to mix in the egg, which we had to add a few

minutes ago. Then you add a dash of milk, a little banana *(Drops the pet frog in and glances at V, who hasn't noticed.)* and mix the mixture with a swoosh of style. *(Mixes so violently that the mixture goes everywhere.)* Before long you have a perfect… well, near perfect cake in the making. Pour out the mixture into a cake tin and pop it in the oven. *(Puts cake mix in cardboard oven.)*

V: That cake's never going to rise!

S: Oh yes it will!

V: Oh no, it won't!

S: Oh yes it will

V: *(Encouraging children to join in.)* Oh no, it won't!

S: Tell you what; let's leave it in the oven a bit whilst we do our song!

S, V and children stand to do the Salt and Vinegar song.

S: Brilliant. Now you look that way, and I'll get the cake out of the oven.

V: Why do I need to look that way?

S: So that when you turn around you can see my gorgeous cake!

V turns around, while S brings out pre-baked cake. V turns back and sees the cake.

V: Wow Salt, it's an amazing cake! *(Pauses, then touches cake.)* It's a bit cold – I thought it would still be hot when it came out of the oven.

S: It's a fan oven.

V: Oh. It's good news though, because we can decorate it now!

S: Great idea!

V: There's a problem.

S: What's that?

V: If this is the big cake for the celebration on Friday, we better make sure we don't mess up!

S: No mistakes.

V: Absolutely no mistakes – we promised Mr Wobbly-jelly, no mistakes!

S: I think we'd better practise at putting the cream on another cake first.

V: I agree.

S: Only problem – we don't have another cake!

V: Tell you what, if I lie down on this table, I can pretend to be the cake and you can decorate me! *(V lies down on table, S covers V's body with a table cloth.)*

S: You ready?

V: Go for it… Plenty of cream just there. *(Points to mouth, S gets plenty on V's face – enough to cover it convincingly.)*

S: I think I should add some sprinkles— *(Freezes as Mr T enters.)*

T: *(Not noticing S and V.)* I am so looking forward to seeing how my young trainee chefs are getting on. Trusting them to make the Celebration Cake was a bit of a risk, but I believe they are capable of creating something special! *(Turns to S.)* Ah Salt, I see you are alone, Vinegar popped out has he… oh look at this… a gorgeous Celebration Cake. I'll have to taste a piece! *(Picks up knife as if to cut it.)*

S: You can't do that!

T: *(Pausing before cutting.)* Why not? It looks delicious!

S: *(Panicking)* Errr, don't you want to keep the cake till Friday?

T: Of course, silly me! I won't have a piece now *(S breathes sigh of relief.)* I'll need the cake for Friday. I'll just taste the cream instead. *(Takes a swipe of cream with a finger and licks it.)* Wonderful, what a beautiful cake – the cream topping is delicious!

V: Thank you.

T: *(Jumping back.)* What? A talking cake?

V: I am a talking cake!

T: Oh my goodness! Salt – you've created a talking cake!

S: *(Unsure.)* Er, yes sir!

T: Unbelievable! I do not believe it! I will have to go and tell my wife. *(Runs off.)* Darling! Sweetikins! You're never going to believe this! Brilliant, totally brilliant!

S: He's gone!

V: I am a talking cake! *(Gets up and starts walking around like a robot.)*

S: How are we gonna get ourselves out of this one? Mr I-believe-in-the-talking-cakey believes we are capable of making a talking cake! If he thinks we can do that, tomorrow's challenge might be even more impossible!

V: We haven't even finished decorating the real cake yet!

S: Well remembered – I think we should decorate this cake out the back, in case he comes back with the carving knife again. See you tomorrow everyone! *(Exits first, taking cake with him.)*

V: *(To the exiting S.)* Hold on Salt – did we get any stickers today? Oh well. *(To audience.)* And another thing, has anyone seen my pet frog? I'll ask Salt! Bye!

SET MENU 4

THE MUSHY PEA CHALLENGE

Props

- Loose garden peas
- Packet of frozen peas
- Some mushy peas
- Two rulers
- Bowl
- Sticking plaster
- Romantic music

Script

S: Good morning everyone!

V: Great to see you!

S: We've got a bit of a problem!

V: I don't know what that yellow box is on the wall! I have a funny feeling that that yellow box is going to turn out to be really important!

S: No, not that problem, we have a sticker problem.

V: Oh – you mean… we only have one and a half stickers, and we need another three and a half! We didn't get any for cake making yesterday.

S: We'll have to cook brilliantly today then. Look, I've found a letter from Mr Buzz-went-the-bee!

V: That's a storming name he's got!

S: Actually, we've had some other great names suggested!

S and V read out some of the names suggested by the children.

V: Brilliant! What does the letter from him say?

S: It says, 'Dear Salt and Vinegar, I still can't believe how amazing you both are – a talking cake – amazing! I think talking cakes are so brilliant, I have decided to award you two Silver Star Stickers each! *(S and V celebrate, before S continues to read.)* I am sorry, I will be out for another eight minutes – I am visiting the Chef Training Scheme Centre to see if any of the other students are capable of making talking cakes! Please can you cook

up some mushy peas for me? I'll be back soon my darlings, lots of love Mr Tagliatelle.'

V: Great news about the stickers – lets do our song!!

S, V and the children do the Salt and Vinegar song.

V: It might be good news about the stickers, but it's a bit worrying that he still thinks we can make talking cakes!

S: We're going to get a bit of a reputation if we're not careful!

V: But today is a new challenge – the making of mushy peas!

S: The making of mushy peas!

V: What is a mushy pea?

S: I think it's a garden pea that has gone mushy.

V: And why would a garden pea go mushy?

S: Maybe it's fallen in love!

V: A garden pea falling in love?

S: Well, imagine you're a handsome pea, and I'm a beautiful pea. We might bump into each other, fall in love and go all mushy inside!

V: So you mean…

S: Yes I mean…

Romantic music plays, S and V run in slow motion towards each other, hamming it up for all they're worth, collide and then hug each other.

V: I'm all mushy!

S: I'm all mushy too!

S and **V**: Oh, we're like two peas in a pod!

They suddenly realise what they're doing, stop and look embarrassed.

S: I've never pretended to be a mushy pea before!

V: Nor have I… *(Pauses.)* So, are you telling me that two garden peas go mushy when they collide?

S: Must be! Mushy peas are created when two garden peas collide.

V: Wow! We need to collide some garden peas then.

Both start looking for peas, S keeps searching without looking at V as V begins to show how desperate he is for the loo!

V: I need a pee!

S: Yes I know, we need some peas!

V: No, I really need a pee!

S: I know we really need some peas.

V: No, I'm totally desperate – I really need a pee.

S: Well I'm getting desperate too – we need to look for at least two peas.

V: I'm really desperate for a real pee!

S: It's OK, I've just found one! *(Picks up a pea.)*

V: Aaarrrrrggghh! *(Dashes off.)*

S: What's wrong with this pea then? It looks like a real pea to me! Where's he gone? *(Stands there bemused. V comes back on stage.)*

V: Gosh, that was close!

S: You back then?

V: Yes.

S: Well, while you've been gone, I've managed to find the garden peas! *(Shows V some loose peas and a packet of frozen peas.)*

V: Great!

S: How can we get the peas to collide?

V: Why don't we have a pea duel!

S: What, with pea guns?

V: No – with two rulers. *(Both pick up a ruler from the table.)*

S: So, if we stand back to back, take four steps, turn and fire, the peas will collide and we shall have two mushy peas.

V: Are you ready! *(S and V stand back to back.)*

S: I'm ready!

As S and V count, they march away from each other.

V: One.

S: Two.

V: Three.

S: Four.

V and S: Fire!

Both turn and launch peas at each other –If either actually gets hit by a pea, they should pretend to die, noisily and theatrically.

S: Well that didn't work very well!

V: I've just had a great idea!

S: How great?

V: Hit-me-over-the-head-with-a-wet-flannel great! We could pretend that the garden peas are grapes, and tread peas like people used to tread grapes and make them go all mushy!

S: Storming idea. Look, here's a big bowl. *(Passes V the bowl that already has mushy peas in it.)* Here are the garden peas. *(Adds them to the bowl.)* Right take off your shoes, Vinegar!

V: Why me?

S: It was your idea!

V: OK! *(Steps into bowl and starts mushing. S takes a good look in the bowl.)*

S: Hey Vinegar, are those your toes?

V: Who else's toes are they going to be?!

S: I didn't realise how hairy your toes are!

V: They remind me of a hobbit every time I look at them!

S: And what's this?

V: Oh, that's my plaster!

S: Your plaster?

V: Yep, I've had a verruca for the last three months!

S: Why's the plaster floating around in the peas?

V: Maybe it's going for a swim!

S: Do plasters like swimming then?

V: I think they must do, you see lots of them in the swimming pool.

S: So you're telling me that you're treading mushy peas with hairy hobbit's feet and a plaster that's gone for a swim?

T: *(Starting to talk off stage, then walking on, talking to children. Vinegar quickly gets out of the bowl, cleans his feet with a towel.)* I can't wait to see those two amazing chefs. Ah, Salt and Vinegar, my super chefs, how have you got on today? *(S and V look worried and freeze to spot as Mr T picks up the bowl.)* Mushy peas in a big bowl… a great idea. Let me taste them. *(Picks up spoon, takes some, maybe showing children, S and V look on shocked.)* Mm – what gorgeous mushy peas! I must take a spoonful to my wife, and then I'll serve the rest to the guests! *(Takes a spoonful and exits.)* Oh those two trainee chefs are fantastic!

S: Oh my goodness he's gonna serve the peas to the guests! What are we gonna do?

S and V: Rescue the plaster! *(They dive into the bowl.)*

V: Got it!

T: *(Coming back in.)* You two are amazing! I congratulate you both on some excellent mushy peas! I have to say this. Of all the chefs we have ever trained here at *Rocky's Plaice*, you two are unique. You are like two peas in a pod! *(S and V look at each other shiftily.)* Tomorrow we've got a big celebration and this kitchen could get very busy! But you two – you seem so sensible – you are capable of culinary miracles. I love you! What

marvellous mushy peas! *(Exits.)*

S and V: Phew!

S: Hold on, he forgot to award us a Silver Star Sticker

V: Mr I-can't-believe-you-didn't-give-us-a-stickery – you didn't give us a sticker!

S: Too late, he's gone. I hope he's not ill after eating our mushy peas.

V: He's probably the first person ever to eat plaster and verruca-flavoured mushy peas!

S: See you tomorrow everyone! Bye!

V: Don't forget those extra names for Mr There's-a-plaster-on-my-tootsie! Oh yes, and I still need to find my pet frog Bananas! *(Starts calling out as he leaves.)* Bananas, Bananas…

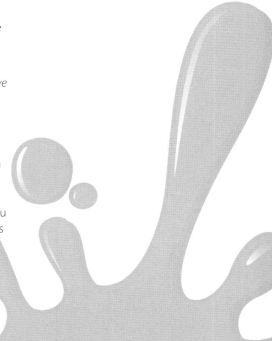

SET MENU 5

THE CELEBRATION

Props

- Cardboard microwave
- Waffle
- Plates
- Yorkshire pudding, onion gravy, apple crumble and custard
- Bread, margarine, ham, cucumber, lettuce, custard, apple pie, mushy peas, gravy, cream, sticking plasters, plastic frog, knife

Script

All 3 chefs arrive at the same time, with Mr T's arms around S and V.

T: So my lovelies – it's up to you two today. I'll have to go and make sure all the guests know the menu and check that the waiters are doing their jobs properly. It's so busy out there! For the first few minutes, you'll be on your own. I am confident you'll do a great job. I'll shout the orders through to you! See you in a bit… Oh, before I go, I need to award you for yesterday's fantastic mushy peas: one more Silver Star Sticker for you… and one for you! *(Exits.)*

S: We only need half a Silver Star Sticker to become Super Star Chefs!

V: Easy-peasy! Let's do our song again!

S, V and the children do the Salt and Vinegar song.

S: That's so cool!

V: You know Mr There's-a-plaster-on-my-tootsie? I honestly can't remember his real name!

S: I think it's Mr Tagliatelle, but lets check out what the children have come up with today!

They read some suggestions out.

V: Those are great names!

T: *(Offstage.)* First order: hot waffle!

S: Hot waffle coming up, Mr Wobbly-jelly! Quick, here's the waffle – bung it in the microwave.

V: How long?

S: Ten seconds

V: Hey Salt, what's this? *(Wiggles little finger to make micro-wave.)*

S: I don't know, what is it?

V: A microwave!

S: *(Pretending to be the microwave.)* Ding!

V: Quick!

S: Ooohhh! *(Juggles the waffle as it's too hot. He throws it to V.)*

V: Wooaah!

They spend a few seconds throwing the waffle between them, then they drop it on the floor.

T: *(Offstage.)* Where's my waffle?

S: Quick here's a plate!

V puts waffle on plate and S takes it off-stage.

V: Phew!

S: *(Coming back on.)* That was close!

T: *(Offstage.)* Second order: Yorkshire pudding and onion gravy; apple crumble and custard.

S: I've got the apple crumble.

V: I've got the onion gravy. *(Pours gravy onto crumble.)*

S: I've got the Yorkshire pudding.

V: I've got the custard. *(Pours custard onto Yorkshire pudding.)*

S: Errr…

V: Very strange!

S: Apple crumble and onion gravy.

V: Yorkshire pudding and custard.

T: *(Offstage.)* Where are my dishes?

V: In the dishwasher!

S: *(Taking the plates offstage.)* Coming!

V: That was a very strange order!

S: *(Coming back on.)* We must have some very strange guests!

T: *(Offstage.)* Third order: chef's special – The Super Sonic Sandwich!

S: Chef's special – The Super Sonic Sandwich. What's that?!

V: I haven't got a clue what a chef's special super sonic sandwich is!

S: I imagine it's a sandwich which has got a bit of everything.

V: Are you sure?

S: Positive.

V: OK, what have we got then?

S: We'll need some bread.

V: OK. *(Puts first piece of bread on plate.)*

S: Next we need… Marg.

V: That's the name of Mr Wobbly-jelly's auntie!

S: No, marg for spreading on bread!

V: Oh. *(Starts to spread.)* What next?

As S calls out the next few ingredients, he runs around finding them and giving them to V. V builds up the layers adding extra slices of bread as appropriate.

S: Ham.

V: Ham!

S: Cucumber.

V: Cucumber!

S: Lettuce.

V: Lettuce!

S: Custard.

V: Are you sure?

S: We said a bit of everything.

V: OK, custard!

S: Apple pie.

V: Apple pie!

S: Mushy peas.

V: Mushy peas!

S: Gravy.

V: Gravy!

S: Cream.

V: Cream!

S: And to finish the sandwich…

V: And to finish the sandwich…

S: Plasters.

V: Plasters – oh they'll love plasters!

S: I hope he's got a big appetite! *(Takes order offstage to Mr T.)*

V: I hope he's got a big mouth!

As S comes back on, the conversation between Mr T and the customer happens offstage.

Customer: Arrrgghh!

T: What's wrong?

Customer: This sandwich has got a plaster in it!

T: Wait till I see those two chefs. Salt! Vinegar!

V: *(Looking worried.)* Now we're for it!

S: We've cooked our goose!

V: Our custard's gone lumpy!

S: Our apple's crumbled!

V: And I still can't find my pet frog Bananas! *(Starts crying.)*

T: *(Shouting.)* RAAAAAAAAARRRR! You… you… you are…

Charlie Chutney: *(Bursting on stage.)* Brilliant!

T: *(Angry and confused.)* Brilliant?

C: Brilliant! Absolutely brilliant!

T: Absolutely rubbish!

C: I disagree! Let me introduce myself. I am Charlie Chutney!

S: Wow! *The* Charlie Chutney?

V: Charlie Chutney, the star of the world-famous *Cooking with Chutney* TV programme!

C: The one and the same! And I've been watching you two in action!

S: Really?

V: How?

C: Through that! *(Points to the camera on the wall.)*

V: Oh you mean that box on the wall? I've been wondering what that is all week. Do you know what it is?

S: It must be a camera, you banana!

V: Oh, I see!

S: Does that mean you've seen everything?

V: Like the time I pretended to be that cake and got decorated?

C: Yep.

S: You saw the plaster when it went swimming in the mushy peas?

C: Yep.

V: You saw Salt batter the fish with my rounders bat?

C: Yep.

T: What on earth are you talking about? The world is going mad!

V: So you saw all the interesting pie combinations?

C: Uh-huh.

S: The cake incident.

C: Uh-huh.

V: The mushy pea controversy.

C: Uh-huh. It's all on film, and I would like to say that you have been terrific! I hereby award you both the final half a sticker – you are indeed Super Star Chefs!

Salt and Vinegar do a celebration dance.

C: Listen guys, you've inspired me. I've decided to start a spectacular new TV show: *Salt and Vinegar's Fish and Chip Takeaway*, and I'd like you two to be the Super Star Chef presenters, what do you say?

S: Salt and Vinegar – Super Star Chefs!

V: Salt and Vinegar – Super Star TV Chefs!

S: We need a manager!

V: We need a manager!

T: *(Depressed.)* I need a new job!

S and V: You can be our manager!

T: *(Excited.)* Magnifico!

S: We need a mascot.

V: We need a mascot.

T: I've found your frog Bananas.

S and V: He can be our mascot! *(Mr T hands V the pet frog.)*

V: Where did you find my lovely Bananas?

T: He was walking down the road, covered in cake mixture, crying out, 'Daddy, Daddy!'

V: *(Cuddling the frog.)* Oh Bananas, my poor little froggy woggy! I've missed you!

S: Hey Vinegar – Bananas is back and we're going to be famous!

V: I think we should celebrate!

S: It's time for a song!

All characters and children do the Salt and Vinegar song, swapping 'TV stars' for 'trainee chefs'.

S: Thank you for all your help everyone.

V: What a day! It's a day of celebration! Come on, we've got a TV show to make! Thank you everyone, bye! Bananas, do you want to be a TV star too?

They all exit, congratulating each other.

SPECIAL MENU B

EPILOGUE

Props

- Two cans of squirty cream
- Victoria sandwich cake
- Protective covering for the church leader

Script

S and V come in dressed in posh clothes.

S: Do you think they'll recognise us?

V: I think they might!

S: Hi everyone!

V: It's time for a song!

All do the Salt and Vinegar Song, substituting the words 'TV stars' for 'trainee chefs'.

Church Leader: Excuse me! Some of the children obviously know you two. The rest of us are wondering who you are.

S: We are Salt and Vinegar – the new hosts of *Salt and Vinegar's Fish and Chip Takeaway*.

V: It's a new Saturday night primetime TV extravaganza live from *Rocky's Plaice*.

CL: So how come you two ended up as TV presenters?

S: Well we started the week as the trainee chefs in *Rocky's Plaice*, and we were set loads of amazing challenges with the aim of earning ourselves five Silver Star Stickers!

If possible, during the next section, photos of the relevant scenes from previous day's episodes are shown.

V: That's right. We needed the five Silver Star Stickers to become Super Star Chefs!

S: We had to make our own chefs' hats.

V: That earned us half a star each.

S: We learnt how to batter a fish!

V: We didn't get any stars for that one, cos we made a bit of a mess of it.

S: We made some ultimate celebration combination pies!

V: Mushroom and toothpaste was my favourite! One star for that.

S: We made the most delicious celebration cake!

V: I was a talking cake! Mr Wobbly-belly thought I was a talking cake – he was so amazed that he gave us two stars each.

S: We also made the most delicious mushy peas.

V: *(As an aside to the church leader.)* Did you know that you make mushy peas by making garden peas collide with each other?

S: Then yesterday it was mad in the kitchen and we had to make loads of dishes really quickly.

V: *(Dramatically.)* And we got the shock of our lives! Just after we delivered a Super Sonic Sandwich, which happened to include some custard and a sticking plaster, we heard this shriek! One of the lovely guests didn't like our sandwich very much. Mr My-legs-are-turning-to-jelly (the head chef) came in furious and was just about to really tell us off, when in came non other than Charlie Chutney, the star of the world famous, *Cooking with Chutney* TV programme! Apparently he'd been watching us all week on a hidden camera and thought that we were hilarious. Amazingly, he's asked us to be the presenters of his new TV show. We might not be brilliant cooks, but we're still Super Star Chefs! He even gave us the extra half sticker we needed!

CL: Well, we are truly honoured to have such TV megastars here in church today!

S: We were actually wondering if you wouldn't mind helping us get ready for our new show.

CL: Me? Of course! Anything I can do to help you two young TV stars.

V: That's great cos we need to practise our presentation skills! The first show is full of really quick cake decoration ideas – we've came up with a great idea for a cake.

S: All you need to do is to hold this Victoria sandwich. *(Hands CL a Victoria sandwich.)*

V: We are going to attempt simultaneous cake decoration whilst talking directly to the audience!

CL: OK!

S and V position themselves either side of church leader

S: *(To V across front of CL.)* I'm just wondering whether it might be best for the boss here to put a robe on so he/she looks like a proper vicar!

V gets robe and puts it on CL.

CL: Are we ready now?

S: We're ready.

V: Three…

S: Two…

V: One…

S: We're live!

During this next section, S and V talk to the audience as if talking into a camera.

V: Ladies and gentlemen, boys and girls, welcome to the first ever edition of our new show *Salt and Vinegar's Fish and Chip Takeaway*.

S: Today, live here in *Rocky's Plaice* we have a willing volunteer.

V: Indeed we have, and with his help we're going to show you how to decorate a Victoria sandwich in 20 seconds!

S: Are you ready – we need a countdown from the audience… 5, 4, 3, 2, 1!

They begin decorating the cake while looking at audience. They make a real mess.

V: *(Looking at audience, while covering the church leader with cream.)* Victoria sandwiches were first made famous by Queen Victoria's pet poodle, Prudence.

S: On the first ever sandwich the cream was plastered on without too much care for where some of it ended up.

V: In fact the first ever Victoria sandwich to be decorated was held over a puddle by Sir Walter Raleigh – unfortunately he got covered in cream.

S: *(To V in front of CL.)* Err, Vinegar.

V: Yes, Salt?

S: Have you seen the church leader?

V: I think he's disappeared!

S: How come the Victoria sandwich is still hanging here then?

V: I don't know. *(Removes some of the cream from the church leader.)*

S: Oops!

V: I think we need a bit more practice!

S: I agree! Thank you very much for your help Mr/Mrs Church Leader.

V: Ladies and Gentlemen, boys and girls, a big hand for Mr/Mrs Church Leader!

S: I think it's time for a hymn or something!

V: How about 'All things bright and creamiful'? Ha, ha! Bye!

S: Bye!

Both exit quickly.

Bible discovery notes

SET MENU 1

With older children: *Rocky's Menu*

Play the game on page 5 and chat about different things you see in the air. Read the story of the Ascension from Acts 1 (from page 6 or a Bible) and see if the children can spot something (or rather, someone) unexpected going up into the sky.

Look at the words on page 7 and, together, try to work out which ones would best describe Jesus' followers. If the children have any words of their own, encourage them to write them in the blank spaces. Crack the code to discover the two promises on page 8 and then chat about how these promises would have made the disciples feel hopeful.

Finally, look at page 10 and ask your group what they hope for and how realistic that hope is. Be prepared to talk about what it means to have hope in Jesus. If you have an appropriate personal story, then share it with your group.

With younger children

Spot the things that shouldn't be in the sky on the *Daily Special* (there are five: flying pig, boy on bike, car, ship, woman in wheelchair). Then retell the story of Acts 1:6–11 or read it from a child-friendly Bible. Read verses 8 and 11 again (they are on the *Daily Special*) and ask the children what they can hear being promised. Say that these two things (the Holy Spirit and Jesus coming back) gave the disciples hope.

Ask the children what they are hoping for. Get them to write or draw it around the word hope on the *Daily Special* (or just on a piece of paper with 'Hope' written in the middle). Talk about hopes that will happen and ones that are less uncertain. Chat about why you have hope in Jesus, and how that hope is certain.

With all ages

Adapt these questions to suit your group, sharing your own feelings, opinions and experiences as appropriate:

- What do you hope for?
- When you have good news who do you like to tell?
- How do you think the disciples felt about telling others about Jesus?
- What do you think of the story of Ascension?
- What do you think might have happened next?

SET MENU 2

With older children: *Rocky's Menu*

Look at the different power sources on page 11 and try to decide what they are. Chat together about which ones the children think they use (they may not know if they use wind or solar power, but they may have seen panels and turbines). Think about how dangerous some power can be, but how useful.

Read the story of Pentecost in Acts 2 (from pages 12 and 13 or a Bible). As you read together, encourage the children to put a fiery shape (using red pens, if you have them) around bits that they think are exciting. Compare exciting sections – this will give you an idea of what the children thought of the story. Ask the group how they would tell others about this story – challenge them to write a postcard to someone (on page 14). What would they say? How would they have felt?

Go on to discover more about the Holy Spirit using page 15 and, if it is appropriate for your church setting, use page 16 to explore the difference the Holy Spirit could make to areas of the children's lives.

With younger children

Read the story of Pentecost from Acts 2:1–11. Use a child-friendly Bible or retell it with your own words (but have a Bible with you so that children know where the story comes from). Look at the three pictures on the *Daily Special* and decide together how Jesus' followers must have felt in each picture. Write those feelings down next to the pictures.

In the story, the Holy Spirit fills Jesus' followers with excitement and courage! Chat with the children about how the Holy Spirit helps and guides you now. Keep your examples simple and appropriate, but be sincere and animated in the telling. If the children are facing any difficult situations or are sad, then write these in the speech bubble and pray together about them.

With all ages

Adapt these questions to suit your group, sharing your own feelings, opinions and experiences as appropriate:

- How many different languages can you name?
- Can anyone in your group speak a foreign language?
- What do you think it would have been like to have been in the crowd at Pentecost?
- What do you think is the most exciting part of this story?
- What do you think of the story of Pentecost?

SET MENU 3

With older children: *Rocky's Menu*
Read Acts 3:1,2. Decorate the Beautiful Gate on pages 20 and 21 and wonder why the man had to beg by the entrance to the Temple. Then go on to read Acts 3:3–10 (from page 22 or a Bible), stopping to draw the man in various states of not being able to walk and walking!

Summarise verses 11 to 21, but talk about verses 12 and 16 in particular, as these focus on the fact that the man had faith in Jesus. Look at page 24 and talk to the children carefully about what it means to have faith. Faith can be used sometimes as a jargony word, but it is an important concept when talking about being a Christian.

Look at page 26 together and chat about the different people we have faith in. Have a silly explanation ready (maybe about having faith in your football team and being let down). Explain that it's good to have faith in some people, but not everybody. Talk about why you have faith in Jesus and how you show this in your everyday life.

With younger children

Decorate the picture of the Beautiful Gate on the *Daily Special*. As you work, tell the children about why beggars sat next to the Temple (they could not work, begging was their only income, people regularly went to the Temple, so there would be lots of people to ask for money).

Read or retell Acts 3:1–11 to the children. Stop at verses 2, 7 and 8 and ask the children to draw the man at these points (verse 2: lying down; verse 7: being helped up; verse 8: jumping about). Crack the code to find out how the man was made better. Explain that the man believed that Jesus could make him better and trusted him to do so. He had faith! If appropriate, give a few examples of when you visibly put your faith in Jesus.

With all ages

Adapt these questions to suit your group, sharing your own feelings, opinions and experiences as appropriate:
- How was the man made better?
- How would his life be different now he could walk?
- Who do you know that is sick that needs Jesus to make them better? Pray for them now.
- How can we put our faith in Jesus?
- What do you think of the story of the man who couldn't walk?

SET MENU 4

With older children: *Rocky's Menu*
Before the session, find out what the names of all the children in your group mean. (Put 'meaning of names' into an Internet search engine.) Using page 28, help the children discover what their names mean if they don't already know. You could turn it into a matching game. Move on to do the clothes picture game on page 29.

Read Acts 9:36–42 (from page 30 or a Bible) and fill in the blank faces on page 31, thinking together about how the people must have felt. Why were the people sad that Dorcas had died? Talk about how Dorcas had showed God's love to them, by making clothes for them (see verse 39). Explain that widows would be very poor, because at that time, it was usually the men who earned money, and they had no man to provide for them.

Go on to think about how you can show God's love to others, chat about appropriate ideas for a while and encourage the children to write down an idea they like.

The session does not concentrate much on the fact that Dorcas was brought back to life by Peter, but the children may well have questions about it. If they'd like to talk about it, then try to answer any questions they have, while not dwelling too long on the subject.

With younger children

Look at the pictures of clothes on *Daily Special*. Can the children tell what they are? (They are: 1 shoes, 2 shirt, 3 T-shirt, 4 trousers, 5 skirt, 6 sunglasses.) Read the story of Dorcas to the children from Acts 9:36–42, or retell it in your own words. Look together at the pictures and decide which picture is most appropriate. Comment that the Bible said Dorcas was always doing good things, so she might have done those other things too!

Encourage the children to write down the names of some of their friends. When they have finished, say a simple prayer thanking God for them, and ask each child to say the names of some of their friends as part of the prayer. Then go on to think about how you could show God's love to those friends. If the children come up with any ideas they'd like to do, then get them to write or draw it in the space provided. The next time you meet, ask the children if they've been able to do it!

With all ages

Adapt these questions to suit your group, sharing your own feelings, opinions and experiences as appropriate:

■ Why were there so many people interested in Dorcas?

■ Why did Dorcas spend so much time making clothes for the poor?

■ Why were people sad that Dorcas had died?

■ What can we do to show other people God's love?

■ What do you think of Dorcas' story?

SET MENU 5

With older children: *Rocky's Menu*

Do the picture puzzle on page 33. If you think it would help, you could go on to explain how the Jews had certain foods that they could and couldn't eat. The picture has 11 animals, six of which were considered unclean (pig, camel, crab, owl, badger, snake) and five which were clean (cow, fish, sheep, chicken, deer). Keep your description brief.

The story of Peter and Cornelius is quite a long one, so you may want to summarise sections of the story. Think about how you're going to do this before the session. Break up the story by reading Acts 10:1–12 to start (from page 34 or a Bible), then draw in the space what Peter saw in his vision. Then read verses 13 to 20 and draw what the Holy Spirit said to Peter. Finally, read verses 21 to 30 and draw what Cornelius saw. As you draw each picture, chat about the story so far.

Solve the maze on page 40 and then use verses 34 to 43 to fill in the missing words on page 41. Chat about Peter's message. The children should have picked up what Jesus did throughout the club, but Peter's words here spell it out clearly. What is the children's response to it? Encourage the children to write what they want to say to God in the two speech bubbles on page 42.

With younger children

The story of Peter and Cornelius is a long one, so you'll need to decide before the session how you're going to retell it more simply for children aged 5 to 8. It's probably not appropriate to read the whole passage from the Bible, but mix up reading with retelling. Make sure you include the episodes illustrated on *Daily Special*. When you have finished your retelling, help the children to reorder the pictures on *Daily Special* so that they are in the order of the story.

Recap what Peter says in Acts 10:34–43, outlining what Jesus has done. They will have heard the good news throughout the club, but it will help for you to go over it here. Ask the children what they think of Peter's message to Cornelius and to write or draw it in the speech bubble. Is there anyone else they'd like to tell about Jesus?

With all ages

Adapt these questions to suit your group, sharing your own feelings, opinions and experiences as appropriate:

■ Have you ever been asked to send a message to someone?

■ What was the angel's message to Cornelius?

■ What was God's message to Peter?

■ How did Peter respond to the message he heard and saw?

■ Is there anyone you'd like to tell about Jesus?

■ What do you think of Cornelius' story?

If any children want to talk to you more about being a friend of Jesus, then there are resources to help you. Page 44 has a simple prayer children can say and page 22 of the *Rocky's Plaice* resource book also has some advice and details of resources for children.

Rocky's Plaice theme song

Dave Godfrey
Arr. Ruth Wills

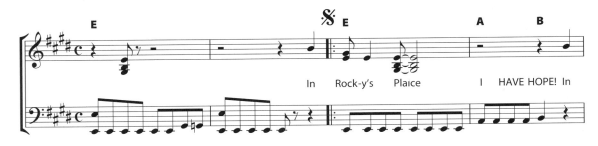

In Rock-y's Plaice   I HAVE HOPE! In

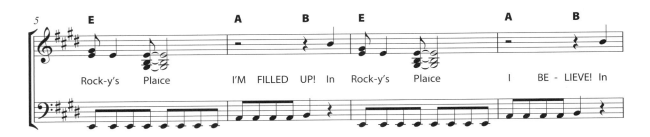

Rock-y's Plaice   I'M FILLED UP! In Rock-y's Plaice   I BE - LIEVE! In

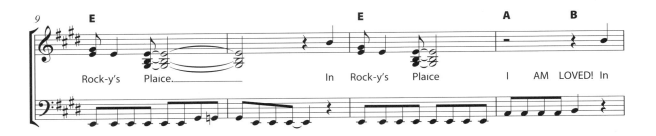

Rock-y's Plaice._____   In Rock-y's Plaice   I AM LOVED! In

Rock-y's Plaice   I TELL THE WORLD! In Rock-y's Plaice   THERE'S GOOD NEWS! In

Rock-y's Plaice._____   (There's) lots of fun__ for ev - 'ry-

© Scripture Union 2009

Learn and remember verse song

Dave Godfrey
Arr. Ruth Wills

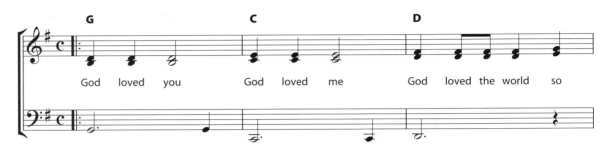

God loved you   God loved me   God loved the world so

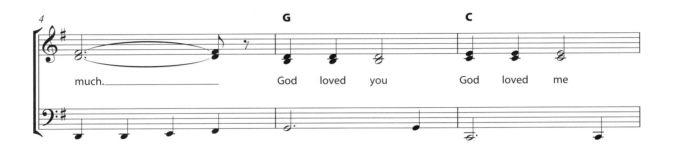

much.____   God loved you   God loved me

God loved the world so much that he sent his

Son.____   Now ev-'ry-one____ who be -

© Scripture Union 2009

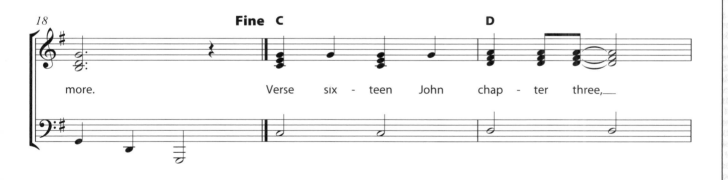

Fifth course Session outlines

Now we're cooking!

Planning your session

When you come to plan each day, make sure you have read the descriptions of the programme in the **First course**. Select the activities according to the children you are likely to have at the club.

You do not need to include all the activities listed here in your programme.

MAKING YOUR CHOICE

There are many factors which will influence your choice of activities:

The children involved

The children should be the most important consideration when choosing the daily activities. Children respond differently to the same activity. Guest Group Leaders in particular should bear this in mind when planning Ice cream crazy.

The length of the club

Simply, if you have a long club, then you will be able to do more! The timings given are merely guidelines; different children will take different lengths of time to complete the same activity. Be flexible in your timings, judge whether it would be more valuable to complete an activity, even though it may be overrunning, rather than cut it short and go on to the next activity. Have something in your programme you can drop if things overrun.

The leaders available

Not every club will be able to find leaders with the necessary skills to fulfil every requirement. If you can't find anyone with a Basic Food Hygiene Certificate, you will have to limit the refreshments you can provide. If you don't have musicians, then you'll have to rely on backing tracks or miss out the singing.

To help Guest Group Leaders prepare for Ice cream crazy, the questions for each day are called Bible discovery notes and can be found on page 45.

Special menu **A** Sunday Service 1

catching the fish

Service outline

Opening worship and prayer

Sing one or two songs of praise to God, including one that tells of God's forgiveness. Go on to pray, asking God to speak to you through his Word and help you as you prepare to share God's Word with the children during *Rocky's Plaice*. The Maitre D' should explain a little about the theme and aims of *Rocky's Plaice*.

Mega game

Explain that every day the Guest Groups will be challenged with a mega game. Ask the congregation to get into small groups and have a go themselves! Display the picture available on the *Rocky's Plaice* website or DVD. Give the congregation 45 seconds to remember all the things connected with a fish and chip restaurant, then 60 seconds in their groups to write down what they can remember.

Songs

Introduce some of the songs you are going to sing during the week. Ask 'The Sardines' to introduce the theme song for the week. This should get everyone in the *Rocky's Plaice* mood!

The Adventures of Salt and Vinegar

Meet Mr Tagliatelle, Salt and Vinegar, and watch Salt and Vinegar's attempt to make their own chef's hats! (See the script on page 31.)

Storytelling

Tell the story of Peter, Jesus and the miraculous catch of fish. This could be done in a variety of ways:

- Ask the person who is going to play Peter at *Rocky's Plaice* to come and tell the story.

Setting the table

KEY STORY
Peter, Jesus and the breakfast on the beach John 21:1–19

KEY THEME
Jesus loves forgiving; Jesus calls Peter to help lead the early church.

KEY POINTS
Jesus' people are a forgiven people, called to love and serve God together. We look forward to the holiday club and set the scene for the week's activities .

- Prepare a set of pictures and use them to illustrate the story as you read John 21:1–19. Two are available on the *Rocky's Plaice* website.
- Use the Dramatised Bible to tell the story, or read while actors act out the story. Try to use different ages and different backgrounds, so the whole church can feel part of the service.

Peter's script
The Church Leader should ask Peter to come and meet the congregation.

Peter: Hi everyone and a massive welcome to *Rocky's Plaice*. My name is Peter, I'm one of Jesus' friends and Jesus trusted me to tell the whole world about him – can you believe it? An ordinary fisherman like me!

Mind you, I thought at one point that I'd completely blown it with Jesus. I was his right-hand man you know, his closest friend for three years. He taught me so many things as we travelled around together. I was an ordinary man, but Jesus made people feel extra-ordinary. That's what he was, and is – extra-ordinary!

Just before Jesus died, I really messed up. Jesus had been arrested and, although I tried to fight the soldiers off, Jesus allowed himself to be taken away. I followed, but when I was asked whether I belonged to Jesus, I was scared. I thought… well I don't really know what I thought – I just told everyone that I didn't even know Jesus. I completely disowned him three times – just when he needed me most.

The great thing with Jesus is that whatever mess we make of our lives, he still loves us and is desperate for us to receive his forgiveness. Several days after Jesus had come back to life I went fishing with some of the other disciples. Don't get me wrong, I was really pleased that Jesus was alive again, but I felt really guilty because I let him down so badly that I wondered if he still wanted to be friends with me. We'd caught nothing that night fishing, and then we heard a voice from the shore, 'Cast your nets on the other side of the boat.' We didn't know who it was, but sometimes you can spot fish from the shore, so we did as he said.

You would not believe the number of fish we caught – we had to get the other boat to come and help us. John whispered in my ear, 'It's Jesus.' I just dived in the sea and swam to him… I just really wanted to be with him…. and yet I still felt so guilty… I needed Jesus, and Jesus knew it. What amazed me was that Jesus actually wanted and needed me!

We had some breakfast together, then Jesus took me to one side and said, 'Simon,' (that's my original name) 'Simon son of John, do you love me more than the others do?' 'Yes, Lord,' I said, 'you know that I love you.' Jesus said, 'Feed my lambs.' Then he said again, 'Simon son of John, do you truly love me?' I answered, 'Yes, Lord, you know that I love you.' Jesus said, 'Take care of my sheep.' The third time he said to me, 'Simon son of John, do you love me?' I was hurt because Jesus had asked me a third time, 'Do you love me?' I said, 'Lord, you know all things; you know that I love you.'

Three times I let Jesus down and three times he gave me the opportunity to tell him I love him! I really was forgiven. But more than that – he'd asked me to feed and look after his sheep, his lambs. Do you know who his sheep and lambs are? That's right – God's people. So much happened after that, and I hope you'll stick around this week so I can tell you some of the stories. Do you know what the last thing Jesus said to me on the beach was? He said to me, 'Follow me!'

Talk

Begin by outlining Peter's relationship with Jesus. (For a summary of Peter's life, see the *Rocky's Plaice* website.) Reinforce what it actually meant for Peter to 'feed my sheep' – he was given the responsibility of looking after Jesus' followers as the good news spread.

Talk about forgiveness – the church is a group of people (note: not a building!) who have turned to God and been forgiven for all their sin. The church is full of ordinary people, like Peter, who love God and want to serve him in the world. We will spend this week in *Rocky's Plaice* – a fish and chip restaurant where God's community meets – a community that loves telling children about Jesus! At *Rocky's Plaice*, we will explore the experiences of the early church and discover for ourselves what it means to be part of God's chosen people. Challenge the congregation to accept and ask for Jesus' forgiveness if there are things not yet sorted out. Do what Peter did – dive in the water and go to Jesus. Conclude by stating that Peter may have been chosen as the leader of the new church, but it was God who was the director! One of Peter's catchphrases is 'God did it' – the story of the early church is a story of God's interaction with ordinary, chosen people.

Encourage the congregation to pray for and support the leaders, helpers and children who will be part of the holiday club this week.

Prayer

Pray for the forthcoming holiday club. This could be done in various ways. You could ask people to pray in small groups or ask the team to come to the front of the hall to be prayed for. Also pray for the children who are coming. Their influence upon their friends who come is as important as any adult input.

Why not, as you pray for the club, ask the congregation to record a special message on video for the children who come to the club? It could then be played in *Rocky's Plaice* at the beginning of **Set menu 1**! The children will hopefully then understand that the whole church is behind the project.

Closing worship

Choose some songs which the congregation knows, to worship God together. Finish by singing the *Rocky's Plaice* song.

Set menu 1
Ascension

In the kitchen

SPIRITUAL PREPARATION

Read together
Read Acts 1:1–11

Talk together
Before sharing the thoughts below, briefly discuss these questions:
- What emotions had the disciples encountered since Palm Sunday?
- What are the key promises stated in this story?

Share together
It must have been hard for Peter and the other disciples to grasp the enormity of the events surrounding them. Peter had been on an emotional rollercoaster. He'd seen his friend and Lord arrested and crucified. He'd then totally betrayed the one he loved. He'd seen Jesus rise from the dead and forgive him at the breakfast on the beach. He'd even been asked by Jesus to lead his church.

The Day of Ascension would have stayed long in his memory. It wasn't a scene of despair – it was a scene of hope. There was hope that Jesus would come again – a hope that the early church clung to during their darkest hours. There was also hope that Jesus would fill each one of them with his Holy Spirit.

Today we are going to share with children the excitement that is building in *Rocky's Plaice*. The children will meet Peter and James who will recount the story of the Ascension. We will also help the children to understand what Christian hope is and how they can share in the same hope enjoyed by the early disciples.

Setting the table

KEY STORY
The Ascension – Acts 1:6–11

KEY THEME
Jesus is coming back one day.

KEY AIMS
- To introduce the children to Peter and the story of the Ascension
- To understand the Biblical concept of hope
- To provide a fast-moving, fun-filled morning which the children will love and which will encourage them to come back tomorrow!

For children with no church background
Hope is something that all children will be familiar with, and this is a good way into this story with children with little or no church background. This is an unusual story, one that many children are not likely to have heard, but reference is made to Jesus' story, which some children may be more familiar with. Highlight this to the children today, but this will be examined in more detail in Set menu 3.

For church children
Some children may be familiar with Ascension as a church festival, but not know what it is all about. Place the story in the context of stories that they may be more familiar with (such as Jesus' resurrection), and help them see how it fits into Jesus' story.

For children from other faiths
This story could be problematic for children of other faiths as, while some traditions believe Jesus' (uncrucified and unresurrected) body was ascended to heaven, others do not - rather that his body is buried on earth. Yet the theme of hope might be drawn out from this story for all – hope of a better future and a better world, of which the children can all be a part.

Pray together
- Pray for the day's activities.
- Pray for the children as they are welcomed.
- Pray for the team, that God will give you everything you need as you serve him today.

PRACTICAL PREPARATIONS

Talk through the morning's programme, and make sure everyone is aware of their responsibilities. Ensure that all resources are ready for the various activities.

Encourage the team to be as welcoming and interactive with the children as possible. Remind them of Jesus' love for children and encourage them to engage with the wonder of the stories. If you are having a Cornelius party at the end of your holiday club, you might like to give parents a letter today that explains a bit about the party so that they can keep the time free.

Equipment checklist for Set menu 1
- **Registration** Registration forms, badges, labels, pens, team lists
- **Guest Groups** Bibles, *Rocky's Menus* or *Daily Specials*, Bible discovery notes, badge-making equipment, fish shapes, pens, felt-tip pens
- **Music** The Sardines band all set up or backing tracks
- **Drama** Costumes and props
- **Technology** PA system, laptop, PowerPoints and projection/OHP and acetates, fish of the day and mega game pictures, *Rocky's Plaice* DVD
- **Activities** Equipment for games and craft
- **Maitre D'** Running order, notes, story chest and boomerang with 'Hope' written on
- **Refreshments** Drinks and biscuits, or other refreshments
- **Storytelling** Costumes for Peter and James

Serving time

As the children arrive and register, play lively music in the background and display the *Rocky's Plaice* logo on the screen to welcome the children.

Have a welcome team on hand to greet the children and take them to their Guest Group. As this is the first day, make sure the welcome desk is well staffed, so that unregistered children and their parents don't have to wait too long.

A TABLE FOR YOU
10 minutes

What you need
- White stickers or circles of white card, safety pins and sticky tape
- Felt-tip pens

What you do
Get to know each other by making name badges. Either use stickers or, for a longer-lasting badge, circles of card with safety pins stuck to the back. (You could use a badge-making machine if you have one.) Encourage the children to write their name on the badge and decorate it as they wish. As you all work, chat and start to get to know the children. The Maitre D'(s) should visit some of the Guest Groups to chat and introduce themselves.

RED HOT!
45 minutes

At this point, bring everyone together in front of the stage area for Red hot! Play music as all the children join the larger group.

The Maitre D'(s) should introduce themselves and welcome everyone to *Rocky's Plaice*. This will include quickly describing some of the activities in store, as well as telling everyone where the toilets and fire exits are. It's important to run through whatever fire procedures you have. Tell them any simple rules you have, such as listening when someone else is talking.

RESTAURANT CLEANING CREW
The cleaning crew leads the cast and crew in a daily 'warm up' session. This will involve simple stretches and aerobics moves in order to bring the whole group together, get everyone loosened up and in the mood for a fun-filled programme.

KEY WORD: HOPE
STORY CHEST: BOOMERANG
Introduce the story chest, explaining that it was found out the back as you were preparing for the holiday club this week. In the chest are special objects that will help us discover each day something special about the first Christian church. Pull out a boomerang and ask the children if they know what it is. Have a creative think together about the boomerang – what might that tell us about the church? Leave it somewhere where it can be seen for the rest of the week. Introduce the children to the key word for the day: hope. State that we are hopeful when we look forward to something that will definitely happen because God has promised it.

FISH OF THE DAY

Introduce Mr Tagliatelle, the head chef of *Rocky's Plaice*. He then tells the children about the fish of the day:

Mr Tagliatelle: Welcome to *Rocky's Plaice* – we have a wonderful selection of beautiful fish for you available on our exclusive menu. Today's special 'Fish of the day' is called the flying fish. *(Show a picture.)*

I have chosen this fish because this amazing fish does something you do not expect fish to do – this fish flies! Fish do not usually take to the air. Amazingly, a film crew from Japan once filmed one of these lovely fish fly for 45 seconds – amazing! I wonder what else you might see fly in the air that you might not expect? Have a beautiful day!

MEGA GAME: 'WHAT'S THAT IN THE SKY?'

Explain the rules of today's mega game to the children and then play it together.

Explain that you are going to show everyone a picture of 15 things to do with the sky and that everyone has 90 seconds to remember in their Guest Groups everything they've seen. Display the picture from page 94 on the screen and allow everyone to see the picture for 30 seconds. In Guest Groups the children then have 90 seconds to remember as many items as possible. Reveal the pictures, one by one, and ask the Guest Group Leaders to check their Group's sheets.

SONGS

Teach the *Rocky's Plaice* song to the children. Encourage the children to sing the words as best they can. Also teach the children suitable actions go with it (suggested actions are on page 26).

RED HOT NEWS

Introduce Captain Ketchup to the children. If CK is a puppet, the Maitre D' may have to stay on stage to show the children how to do the ketchup dance!

Captain Ketchup: Good morning everyone, and welcome to Red Hot News! It's time to do the ketchup dance! (Everyone does the ketchup dance. See the *Rocky's Plaice* website.) Thank you! This is Red Hot News – helping you ketch-up with the news! Ooh, it's hot!

The Red Hot News today is that there may be a party here on the last day of *Rocky's Plaice*. Hurrah! I can't wait for the party rings – they're my favourite biscuits. I think the bit in the middle is the best bit!

Hot News! There are two new trainee chefs in the restaurant today – I know the boss has big hopes for them both – I'm sure you'll meet them later!

Hot News! There are some great fishy activities lined up for you, our lovely guests, here, at *Rocky's Plaice*!

Hot News! Edna, my pet hamster, has finally given birth to two gerbils!

Hot News! The key word for today is hope: hope is looking forward to something that will definitely happen because God has promised it.

Hot News! Peter, a friend of Jesus, has just arrived. I think he's heading your way.

Maitre D': That's great news CK, we'll see you tomorrow. Peter is here! We can ask him about the boomerang! Big clap for Captain Ketchup! Boys and girls, a big welcome for Peter!

(You will need to amend this last section of Red Hot News if you are using the DVD rather than the Peter storytelling.)

STORYTELLING

Welcome Peter on stage and perform this script. Alternatively, introduce the DVD and show episode 1 to the children. You might be using both, in which case, show the DVD after Peter and James have left the stage.

Maitre D': Hi Peter, it's great to see you! Boys and girls, this is Peter – he told people about Jesus and helped the first churches to start.

Peter: Hi everyone, it's great to see you in *Rocky's Plaice*!

Maitre D': Peter, we've discovered this story chest, and we've got the first object out… it's a boomerang and apparently it's something to do with what happened to the first Christians. Can you help us?

Peter: Oh, the old boomerang story! It's a great story that one, I'll tell it to you in a mom—

James: Peter, is that really you?

Peter: *(Surprised.)* James! Boys and girls may I introduce you to James – he was one of Jesus' disciples, just like me. He used to lead the church in Jerusalem.

James: Morning everyone. What are you up to Peter?

Peter: I'm just about to tell the children the boomerang story!

James: The boomerang story! Oh, it was an amazing day that one! A boomerang is a great way of remembering it. If you throw a boomerang away, it comes back to you.

Peter: The boomerang story is the story of the day Jesus went back to heaven. We'd lived with him for three years, seen him do amazing miracles, heal the sick and raise the dead. We'd heard his stories and his wonderful teaching. We'd lived with him and learnt so much about God's wonderful love. We saw him arrested and then crucified

– he was killed on a cross. Then, three days later he appeared to us – alive again! God did it! God brought him back to life! He appeared to many people – in fact at one point he appeared to over 500 people at the same time!

James: I remember it well – I was there.

Peter: He then had some private chats with us, his disciples, including one chat where he told us to wait in Jerusalem until we received the Holy Spirit, so that we could tell the whole world about Jesus. Then, in front of our eyes (we were up a bit of a hill), Jesus just went up into the air, into the clouds and disappeared. We know it was the last time we'd see him for a while. Do you remember the angels, James?

James: Those fantastic, massive, beautiful, strong and handsome angels of God. I love it when I see angels! Yes I remember them – they told us something that fills us all with HOPE.

Peter: Hope is the key word on the boomerang!

James: I keep thinking about what the angels said. *(Asks the children.)* Do you want to know what the angels said? Well, we were all gazing up into the sky, and these angels appeared and said, 'Why are you men from Galilee standing here and looking up into the sky? Jesus has been taken to heaven. But he will come back in the same way that you have seen him go.'

Peter: Boomerang! Jesus is coming back! He's not come back yet though, but he will do one day. That's the hope of the church.

James: What was the name you came up with for the time Jesus went into heaven?

Peter: We call it the Ascension. Ascend means to go up. It was Ascension Day!

James: That's a great story, what an amazing day!

Peter: Yes, such a fantastic day.

They walk off chatting excitedly to each other, just remembering to say goodbye to the children before they leave.

MAITRE D'S RECOMMENDATIONS

Thank Peter and James. Remind the children of the key word for the day: hope. Pick up on Peter's words about Jesus, who was God coming to Earth as a man 2,000 years ago. Jesus did lots of teaching, healing, loving and amazing miracles. Though the disciples would have been sad that Jesus had gone back into heaven, they did have hope. They had hope because God had made some wonderful promises about Jesus coming back!

SONGS

After the story, it might be appropriate to sing a song to reinforce the teaching. For example:

- 'God's promises' *Light For Everyone* (SU)
- 'Jesus is the same' *kidsource 2* (world wide worship)

After the songs, announce who the Dish of the Day is later on, and encourage the groups to think of questions to ask the team member. Send everyone to their groups to explore the Ascension more.

ICE CREAM CRAZY
45 minutes

THE REFRESHMENT ZONE

In groups, have your refreshments together, and chat about the club so far. This will give you a good idea about what the children are enjoying. Remind the children to think about questions to ask the Dish of the Day! Go on to explore the Bible together.

LUKE'S SCROLLS

With older children

Play the game on page 5 and chat about different things you see in the air. Read the story of the Ascension from Acts 1 (from page 6 or a Bible) and see if the children can spot something (or rather, someone) unexpected going up into the sky.

Look at the words on page 7 and, together, try to work out which ones would best describe Jesus' followers. If the children have any words of their own, encourage them to write them in the blank spaces. Crack the code to discover the two promises on page 8 and then chat about how these promises would have made the disciples feel hopeful.

Finally, look at page 10 and ask your group what they hope for and how realistic that hope is. Be prepared to talk about what it means to have hope in Jesus. If you have an appropriate personal story, then share it with your group.

With younger children

Spot the things that shouldn't be in the sky on the *Daily Special* (there are five: flying pig, boy on bike, car, ship, woman in wheelchair). Then retell the story of Acts 1:6–11 or read it from a child-friendly Bible. Read verses 8 and 11 again (they are on the *Daily Special*) and ask the children what they can hear being promised. Say that these two things (the Holy Spirit and Jesus coming back) gave the disciples hope.

Ask the children what they are hoping for. Get them to write or draw it around the word hope on the *Daily Special* (or just on a piece of paper with 'Hope' written in the middle). Talk about hopes that will happen and ones that are less uncertain. Chat about why you have hope in Jesus, and how that hope is certain.

With all ages
Adapt these questions to suit your group, sharing your own feelings, opinions and experiences as appropriate:
- What do you hope for?
- When you have good news who do you like to tell?
- How do you think the disciples felt about telling others about Jesus?
- What do you think of the story of Ascension?
- What do you think might have happened next?

CRAFT AND GAMES
Choose a craft activity for today, along with a selection of games that would be suitable for your club. Craft and games activities are on pages 27 to 29. For extra ideas, see *Ultimate Craft* (SU, 978 1 84427 364 5) and *Ultimate Games* (SU, 978 1 84427 365 2).

EXTRA MEATY!
25 minutes

Welcome everyone back by singing a song you have already sung during the session.

THE SIZZLER
Ask the question, 'What things are you hoping for in the future?' and give some time for the Guest Groups to chat about it. Then get some feedback. Discuss some of the children's answers, and help them to understand that some of these hopes are:
- Wishful thinking
- Might happen
- Will definitely happen!

Remind the children that Christian hope is of the 'Definitely happen' variety! Ask the children if they can remember the things that Jesus and the angels said would definitely happen:
- Jesus would come back one day.
- Jesus would take them to be with him in heaven.
- Jesus would send the Holy Spirit.

Encourage the children that God is great at making promises – these promises are true for today too! God has promised that Jesus will come back and that he is preparing a place for everyone in heaven. Also God promises the Holy Spirit – we'll talk about that promise tomorrow! Be encouraged – God loves promising things and we can have HOPE because we can trust God!

DEEP FAT FRYER
Introduce the Deep Fat Fryer, who should come on and tell a few suitable silly jokes that have been prepared before the session. The Deep Fat Fryer should encourage the children to bring in some jokes and pictures for them to read about. The Deep Fat Fryer explains to the children about Scraps the restaurant dog that usually helps them, but today is poorly. Encourage the children to draw some great fun-filled pictures of Scraps as a poorly dog. The children should put their name and group on their jokes or pictures and put them in the special chip-pan basket or bin when they arrive for the next session.

LEARN AND REMEMBER VERSE
Introduce the memory verse for the week: John 3:16. Explain that you'll be learning more about what this verse means at *Rocky's Plaice*. If you are using the song, start to teach it to the children.

Photocopy the Learn and remember verse onto card (you could use the template on the *Rocky's Plaice* website or DVD), then chop it up and give it to the groups as a jigsaw puzzle. In Guest Groups, the children learn the verse – they should be ready to tell the rest of the club what they have learnt!

DISH OF THE DAY
Invite one of the team to talk to the children about the time when they became a friend of God, and how that affected their life and view of the world. Before the session, make sure this is a simple story and one that the children can relate to. Ask the team member one or two of the children's questions too.

THE ADVENTURES OF SALT AND VINEGAR
Introduce the drama, which uses the script from pages 32 to 33. The children meet Salt and Vinegar, trainee chefs at *Rocky's Plaice*.

EXTRA MEATY FINALE!
Quickly ask what the children have enjoyed at *Rocky's Plaice* and then include those things in a short prayer of thanks. Sing the *Rocky's Plaice* song and send the groups to the Get your coats time.

GET YOUR COATS
10 minutes

As you sit in your groups for the final time today, chat about the highlights of the day. Then use the following prayer activity.

CREATIVE PRAYER (HOPE)

What you need
- Fish shapes cut out of paper
- Felt-tip pens
- Blu-tack, drawing pins or sticky tape

What you do

Encourage the children that God loves to hear their prayers! Tell the children that you are going to make a fish display of prayers based on hope. Give each child a cut-out fish shape and something to write or draw with. Ask the children to write or draw a prayer on their fish. It could be a thank you prayer for the session at *Rocky's Plaice*; it could be something they are hoping for during this week or something that they would like God to do for them this week. Tell the children that they do not need to write their names on their fish. When everyone has finished, stick the fish up in the Guest Group area and lead the children in a prayer thanking God for hope and for the first session at *Rocky's Plaice*.

Remind the children about the chip pan and the times for the next session. Guest Group Leaders should know how the children in their group are getting home.

TEAM CLEAR-UP
30 minutes

Have a time where the team can clear up as soon as the children have gone. Then meet for a short time to debrief. Ask for any comments. You could use the traffic light system of green (great), amber (could do better) and red (didn't work) to decide if anything needs reworking for tomorrow. End with a time of prayer. You could break into Guest Groups, with leaders and assistants praying for the children in their group. Finally, make sure any necessary preparation for tomorrow is taken care of. Teams who have their own children with them will want to get away quickly, but do include them in a short debrief and prayer time.

PHOTOCOPIABLE PAGE

ROCKY'S Plaice Set menu **1**

Daily special

Look at this picture. Can you find the five things in the sky that shouldn't be there?

Peter and the rest of Jesus' friends saw Jesus go up to heaven in a cloud. That must have been strange, but they were given two things to look forward to. Read verses 8 and 11 to find out what those promises were!

ACTS 1:8
But the Holy Spirit will come upon you and give you power. Then you will tell everyone about me in Jerusalem, in all Judea, in Samaria, and everywhere in the world.

ACTS 1:11
They said, "Why are you men from Galilee standing here and looking up into the sky? Jesus has been taken to heaven. But he will come back in the same way that you have seen him go."

What do you hope for? Write it down here!

hope

Ask your Guest Group Leader what they hope for.

Set menu 2
Pentecost

Setting the table

KEY STORY
Pentecost – Acts 2:1–18

KEY THEME
Jesus offers the Holy Spirit to his followers.

KEY AIMS
- To introduce the children to God the Holy Spirit and the story of Pentecost
- To understand the biblical concept of being filled with the Holy Spirit

For children with no church background
This is a great story of God's power and you might reflect on the awesomeness of this with children with little or no church background. God the Holy Spirit enabled Jesus' friends to do so much. The idea of something 'living in' or 'filling you up' may be problematic, as this is an alien idea to anyone from outside the church community. Be careful with your jargon and decide what the children in your group will understand.

For church children
Church children may think about this story every year, but not fully understand what God is doing here. Talk about the Holy Spirit enabling Jesus' friends to do so much, and how the Holy Spirit is for all of Jesus' friends.

For children from other faiths
The symbol of fire is a key part of this story. Children of other faiths will understand and recognise similar symbolism from their own traditions, such as the festivals of Diwali (light) and Holi (water/fire) for Hindus and Sikhs.

In the kitchen

SPIRITUAL PREPARATION

Read together
Read Acts 2:1–18.

Talk together
Before sharing the thoughts below, briefly discuss these questions:
- What immediate impact did the coming of the Holy Spirit have on these Christians?
- What long-term impact has the coming of the Holy Spirit had for Christians?

Share together
It must have been difficult for Peter to grasp exactly what Jesus meant when he promised the Holy Spirit to the disciples. When the Holy Spirit came, it must have blown the disciples away! God loved each one of them so much that he was willing to give himself to them (Luke 11:13).

When we are filled with the Holy Spirit, he gives us power to be his witnesses (Acts 1:8). He changes people to be like Jesus (Galatians 5:22,23). God the Holy Spirit also gives special spiritual gifts to his people (1 Corinthians 12:1–11). Having God the Holy Spirit inside each person totally transformed the disciples, and suddenly God was doing miracles through them and empowering them to serve their risen Saviour!

When Peter preached on the Day of Pentecost, he reminded everyone of the prophecy in Joel (Joel 2:28–32) where God promised the Holy Spirit to the nation of Israel. Jesus describes the Holy Spirit as a helper and so much more (John 14:15–31). Jesus said that God would give the Holy Spirit to everyone who asks. Have you asked, and do you continue to ask God to fill you with his Holy Spirit?

Note: Different Christians have slightly different views about the role of the Holy Spirit. Look carefully at the material for this session and adapt it accordingly.

Pray together
- Pray for each other to be filled with the Holy Spirit.
- Pray for the day's activities.
- Pray for the children. Ask God to show the children who he really is and to help them to understand the Day of Pentecost.

PRACTICAL PREPARATIONS
Talk through the morning's programme, and make sure everyone is aware of their responsibilities. Ensure that all resources are ready for the various activities. Encourage the team to be really welcoming and as interactive with the children as possible. If you are having a Cornelius party on **Set menu 5**, give out letters to any parents that weren't around yesterday.

Equipment checklist for Set menu 2
- **Registration** Registration forms, badges, pens, team lists, any information for parents
- **Guest Groups** Bibles, *Rocky's Menus* or *Daily Specials*, pens, Bible discovery notes, paper and art materials, glass, jug of water, plastic covering
- **Music** The Sardines band all set up or backing tracks
- **Drama** Costumes and props
- **Technology** PA system, laptop, PowerPoints and projection/OHP and acetates, fish of the day and mega game pictures, *Rocky's Plaice* DVD
- **Activities** Equipment for craft and games
- **Maitre D'** Running order, notes, story chest and torch with 'be filled' written on
- **Refreshments** Drinks and biscuits, or other refreshments
- **Storytelling** Costumes for Peter and Priscilla

Serving time
As the children arrive, play lively children's music in the background and display the *Rocky's Plaice* logo on a screen using a data projector or OHP. Register any new children and take them to their groups.

A TABLE FOR YOU
10 minutes

GROUP POSTER

What you need
- Large sheet of paper
- Felt-tip pens, paint, collage materials etc

What you do
Work together to create a giant poster for your Guest Group area. Encourage children to draw their favourite meals or things you might see in a restaurant. Or you could decorate the poster with the things children have already seen at *Rocky's Plaice*. As you work, talk about the club so far and what the children have enjoyed. Remind them to put any jokes or pictures for the Deep Fat Fryer into the chip pan!

RED HOT!
45 minutes

Play the *Rocky's Plaice* song as the Guest Groups come together as a big group. Welcome the children to *Rocky's Plaice* and especially welcome any new children. Check to see if the children can remember **Set menu 1**'s key word – hope.

RESTAURANT CLEANING CREW
Introduce the cleaning crew, who lead the children in the daily warm up. Include many of the same exercises as yesterday, but include one or two new ones.

KEY WORD: BE FILLED
STORY CHEST: TORCH
Remind the children about the story chest and point out the boomerang from yesterday. Bring out a torch and ask the children what it is (ask younger children the question). Have a creative think together about the torch – what might that tell us about the church? How does it link to the key word? Place the torch next to the boomerang. Introduce the children to the key word for the day: be filled. Today's story looks at the time when the Christians were first filled with God and his power!

FISH OF THE DAY
Introduce Mr Tagliatelle, who then tells the children about the fish of the day:

Mr Tagliatelle: Welcome to *Rocky's Plaice* – we have a wonderful selection of beautiful fish for you available on our exclusive menu. Today's special fish of the day is called the pufferfish. (*Show a picture.*)

I have chosen this fish because, when it is scared, it fills itself up with water and grows to twice or three times its size! This is not usual fish behaviour, but it helps them to avoid being eaten by bigger fish. I wonder what else you will hear today about being filled up. I hope your day is full of beautiful things!

MEGA GAME: 'WHAT'S THE FILLING?'

Explain the rules to the children and then play the game as described below:

Say that you're going to show a picture of six jars or bottles which are filled with different types of food or drink. The children have to guess from what they can see, and from the types of jars, what each filling is! Display the picture from page 94 and give the guest groups two minutes to decide what each one is. Guest Group Leaders should write the answers down. When two minutes is up, give out the answers and ask Guest Group Leaders to check their group's answers.

Alternatively, give each Guest Group six jars that contain six different foods. The children have two minutes to try and identify all the different foods, without tasting them.

SONGS

Ask the band to lead the children in the *Rocky's Plaice* theme song, together with the actions. In addition, sing a song that was popular yesterday, together with a new one for today.

RED HOT NEWS

Introduce Captain Ketchup and Red Hot News.

Captain Ketchup: Good morning everyone, and welcome to Red Hot News! It's time to do the ketchup dance! *(Everyone does the ketchup dance.)* Thank you! This is Red Hot News – helping you ketch-up with the news! Ooh, it's hot!

The Red Hot News today is that rumours are building about the party here on the last day of *Rocky's Plaice*. Hurrah! I can almost smell those party rings… I totally adore the yellow ones. Once I filled the middle with a massive dollop of cream – it was delicious!

Hot News! Salt and Vinegar will be back in the kitchen later, after a bit of an ear-battering from Mr Wobbly belly!

Hot News! There are more storming activities lined up for you today!

Hot News! Edna, my pet hamster, has named her two gerbils Ant and Dec!

Hot News! The key word for today is 'be filled'. It's actually two words, but I'm not counting! Being filled is what my sandwich was this morning – a beautiful peanut butter and tomato ketchup sandwich!

Hot News! Peter is here again! And that's the news this morning!

Maitre D': That is great news, CK – we'll see you tomorrow. Big clap for Captain Ketchup! Boys and girls, a big welcome for Peter!

(Remember to change the ending of Red Hot News if you are using the DVD instead of the Peter storytelling.)

STORYTELLING

Welcome Peter on stage and perform this script. Alternatively, introduce the DVD and show episode 2 to the children. You might be using both; in which case, show the DVD after Peter and Priscilla have left the stage.

Peter walks in carrying a glass, bowl and jug of water.

Maitre D': Hi Peter, it's great to see you again!

Peter: Hi everyone, it's great to see you in *Rocky's Plaice*.

Maitre D': Peter, yesterday we had a boomerang and you told us the story of the Ascension. Today we've got a torch! Have you got another story for us?

Peter: Oh, the torch story! It's a great story too. I'll tell it to you in a moment. Let me just put these things down. *(Peter puts his props down and the Maitre D' hands him the torch.)* Good morning everyone, and a massive hi to those of you I didn't meet yesterday. My name is Peter. I was one of Jesus' friends and was involved in the first-ever church!

Priscilla: Hi Peter!

Peter: Priscilla! *(Greets her with a hug.)* Take a seat! Priscilla, these *(Introduces Priscilla to the children.)* are some of our lovely guests this week in *Rocky's Plaice*. Children, this is Priscilla – one of the first Christians like me! I was just about to tell the torch story Priscilla!

Priscilla: The torch story – the Day of Pentecost! I was there with you!

Peter: It was the day when the church was filled up with power, like a battery going inside a torch. It was the day the church started!

Priscilla: There were just 120 of us who belonged to Jesus. Yes, just 120 or so of us. We were waiting for the Holy Spirit.

Peter: That's right. Jesus had told us that we should wait in Jerusalem till God sent his Holy Spirit. So all 120 of us waited upstairs in a room.

(To the children.) If you're wondering who the Holy Spirit is, he's the Spirit who is God. He is God who comes and lives in us. God fills us with his Spirit. He changes us to be like him, gives us special gifts and gives us the power to tell the world about Jesus.

Priscilla: That's right, God did it! He filled us with power! We just didn't know what to do, but the Holy Spirit came and changed all that! Anyway, it was only about 9 o'clock in the morning, when the Holy Spirit came. It was the most amazing event. Do you remember it Peter?

Peter: I do, I do – keep going!

Priscilla: Well, we were standing praying, when suddenly there was the sound of a massive wind. I looked up, startled, and yet at the same time I could feel this excitement in me, joy, goosebumps… I knew it was God straight away. Then when I looked at the other people in the room, suddenly there were flames, special flames – well they looked like flames coming out of the head of each person in the room. Then, the room was suddenly filled with praises, shouts, screams of excitement! More than that, suddenly we found ourselves speaking in languages we didn't even know! *(During the next line Priscilla should pick up a glass and pour the water into it until it overflows.)* It was God – filling us up with his Holy Spirit and then overflowing everywhere!

Peter: We couldn't contain ourselves could we? We ran out of the door in to the street and started telling all the people about Jesus!

Priscilla: There were thousands of people there from all over the world. We started talking to them in loads of different languages. Do you know what language God gave me Peter?

Peter: I can't remember; tell us!

Priscilla: I spoke in Egyptian! It was amazing… Mind you, people had heard the noise and now they heard their languages – they couldn't understand what was happening – until you told them Peter.

Peter: That's right; some people actually thought we were drunk with wine! I stood up and told everyone that this was God – he'd promised that he'd send his Spirit to fill up his people, and he'd done it!

Priscilla: How many people became Christians that day?

Peter: It was about 3,000, Priscilla, and the great news is that more people every day are still being added to the church. That day the church was born – it was a wonderful day! I call it the Day of Pentecost – because that was the Jewish festival everyone had come to Jerusalem for. What a great day!

Priscilla: It was one of the best days!

Peter: The Day of Pentecost – the torch day! Oh, and the promise of the Holy Spirit is for you too! I hope to see you tomorrow. God bless. Bye!

The go off chatting excitedly to each other.

MAITRE D'S RECOMMENDATIONS

Thank Peter and Priscilla. Remind the children of the key word for the day: be filled. Ask the children to tell you the link between the story and the torch. Jesus' friends were waiting; they weren't sure what was going to happen next. Then God sent the Holy Spirit and everything changed! They were filled up and told loads of people about God. That's something of what the Holy Spirit does. He can help us tell our friends about Jesus. He can also help us to be more like Jesus and show us how to live more like him.

SONGS

After the song it might be appropriate to sing another song to explore the theme more.
- 'Deep love' *Light For Everyone* (SU)
- 'No more waiting' John Hardwick

After the story, announce who the Dish of the Day is later on, and encourage the groups to think of questions to ask the team member. Send everyone to their groups to explore Pentecost more.

ICE CREAM CRAZY

45 minutes

THE REFRESHMENT ZONE

In your groups, have your refreshments together, and chat about the club so far. Remind the children to think about questions to ask the Dish of the Day, and to bring in jokes and pictures for the Deep Fat Fryer's chip pan!

LUKE'S SCROLLS

With older children

Look at the different power sources on page 11 and try to decide what they are. Chat together about which ones the children think they use (they may not know if they use wind or solar power, but they may have seen panels and turbines). Think about how dangerous some power can be, but how useful.

Read the story of Pentecost in Acts 2 (from pages 12 and 13 or a Bible). As you read together, encourage the children to put a fiery shape (using red pens, if you have them), around bits that they think are exciting. Compare exciting sections – this will give you an idea of what the children thought of the story. Ask the group how they would tell others about this story – challenge them to write a postcard to someone (on page 14). What would they say? How would they have felt?

Go on to discover more about the Holy Spirit using page 15 and, if it is appropriate for your church setting, use page 16 to explore the difference the Holy Spirit could make to areas of the children's lives.

With younger children

Read the story of Pentecost from Acts 2:1–11. Use a child-friendly Bible or retell it with your own words (but have a Bible with you so that children know where the story comes from). Look at the three pictures on the *Daily Special* and decide together how Jesus' followers must have felt in each picture. Write those feelings down next to the pictures.

In the story, the Holy Spirit fills Jesus' followers with excitement and courage! Chat with the children about how the Holy Spirit helps and guides you now. Keep your examples simple and appropriate, but be sincere and animated in the telling. If the children are facing any difficult situations or are sad, then write these in the speech bubble and pray together about them.

With all age groups

Adapt these questions to suit your group, sharing your own feelings, opinions and experiences as appropriate:

- How many different languages can you name?
- Can anyone in your group speak a foreign language?
- What do you think it would have been like to have been in the crowd at Pentecost?
- What do you think is the most exciting part of this story?
- What do you think of the story of Pentecost?

CRAFT AND GAMES

Choose a craft activity for today, along with a selection of games that would be suitable for your club. Craft and games activities are on pages 27 to 29. For extra ideas, see *Ultimate Craft* (SU, 978 1 84427 364 5) and *Ultimate Games* (SU, 978 1 84427 365 2).

EXTRA MEATY!

25 minutes

Welcome everyone back together by singing a song you have already sung during the session.

THE SIZZLER

Ask the question, 'What is the greatest filling ever in a sandwich?' and give the Guest Groups a minute to discuss it. Check out a few of the answers, then finish by stating that we are like a sandwich in the sense that we can be filled! Peter and the other disciples were, and Christians today are filled with the Holy Spirit!

State again for the children what happens when Jesus gives us his Holy Spirit. (You could use the pictures on the *Rocky's Plaice* website or DVD.)

- **Present**: The Holy Sprit gives us special gifts and abilities to help us serve God.
- **Battery**: The Holy Spirit gives us the power to live for Jesus.
- **Jesus**: The Holy Spirit helps us become like Jesus.
- **God**: The Holy Spirit is God who comes and lives in people who follow Jesus.

Read Jesus' promise in Luke 11:10 where Jesus promises the Holy Spirit to anyone who asks him. The Holy Spirit is a good gift!

DEEP FAT FRYER

Welcome the Deep Fat Fryer. Ask them to read out some of the jokes from the children and show some of the pictures of Scraps. The Deep Fat Fryer should thank the children, before telling them why Scraps can't join them today – he's eaten too much, his stomach is full and he's feeling a bit poorly! The Deep Fat Fryer should ask the children to draw a picture of the massive breakfast Scraps ate this morning!

LEARN AND REMEMBER VERSE

If you are using the song, sing it through again. If you think the children are confident with the words, show them the verse with a few words missing and see if they can still sing the whole song.

Alternatively, put each word on a balloon and get some volunteers to hold them in the right order. Say the verse and then gradually pop them as the children repeat it, until they can remember the verse unaided.

DISH OF THE DAY

Invite the Dish of the Day to talk to the children about what the Holy Spirit means to them, and how he helps them in their daily life. Before the session, make sure this is a simple story and one that the children can relate to. Ask the team member one or two of the children's questions too.

THE ADVENTURES OF SALT AND VINEGAR

Introduce the next episode of the drama – the script for this is on page 34. After yesterday's disaster, Salt and Vinegar set about making pies!

EXTRA MEATY FINALE!

Finish off the session by saying thanks to God for all the things you have done together at *Rocky's Plaice* and pray about the rest of the day. Sing the *Rocky's Plaice* theme song to round off Extra meaty! and send the groups to their Get your coats time.

GET YOUR COATS

10 minutes

As you gather in your group for the final time today, chat about the highlights of the day, then go on to the prayer activity.

CREATIVE PRAYER

What you need
- Glass
- Jug of water
- Sheet of plastic and cloth

Give the children a few moments to think and to be quiet. Spread the plastic sheet out and put the glass on top. Start to pour water into the glass until it overflows and as you do so, ask the children to think about God the Holy Spirit and all he does. Finish with an 'out loud' prayer, thanking God for sending the Holy Spirit.

If there is any time left, you could finish *Daily Specials* or any pages from *Rocky's Menu*. Alternatively, carry on with your Guest Group poster from A table for you.

TEAM CLEAR-UP

30 minutes

Have your clear-up time, then meet to debrief. Ask for any comments to evaluate the day. To help you there is an evaluation form on the *Rocky's Plaice* website and DVD. Use the form to review each section of the day. Have a time of prayer and then finish by doing any necessary preparation for tomorrow.

PHOTOCOPIABLE PAGE

ROCKY'S Plaice Set menu 2

Daily special

Listen to the story of Pentecost, when God sent the Holy Spirit!

Look at these pictures and decide how you think Jesus' friends felt in every picture.

VERSE 1

VERSES 2 and 3

VERSE 4

_____

_____

_____

_____

_____

_____

The Holy Spirit is God with us. He helps us make the right choices, teaches us and comforts us when we are sad.

Is there anything you'd like God's help with?

Anything you'd like to tell God about?

Write or draw it in this speech bubble.

Set menu 3
The man who couldn't walk

In the kitchen

SPIRITUAL PREPARATION

Read together
Read Acts 3:1–16.

Talk together
Before sharing the thoughts below, briefly discuss these questions:

- On what basis does the passage say the man was healed?
- How would you describe to a child what the word faith really means?

Share together
Peter and John had no money, but they did have tremendous treasure! They gave to the man riches he hadn't dreamed possible. The man was healed through the power of the Holy Spirit, in the name of Jesus.

You could say that faith involves both believing and trusting. I could believe the doctor can perform the operation. It is another thing to go under anaesthetic and actually trust him that you'll come through the operation safely. By allowing him to perform the operation means that I'm putting my faith in him – both believing and trusting. And that faith will affect the way that I live.

So when someone says they believe in Jesus and their actions show no sign of faith – they do not truly believe. Peter went on to tell the crowds that surrounded him to put their faith in Jesus. He even had the opportunity to tell the Jewish leaders by whose power the man was healed!

Setting the table

KEY STORY
Peter and John heal a man who couldn't walk – Acts 3:1–21 (and John 3:16)

KEY THEME
Faith in Jesus brings eternal life.

KEY AIMS
- To tell the story of the healing of the man who couldn't walk by Peter and John
- To understand the biblical concept of having faith!

For children with no church background
The most amazing part of this story for children with little or no church background is that a man was healed and could walk. Wonder with the children at this, but also think about the fact that Peter and John didn't do this themselves – they did it through the power of Jesus!

For church children
With children from a church community, think about how the man was healed – God did it through Peter and John. Start linking the stories together: the hope of the promise in **Set menu 1** is fulfilled in the coming of the Holy Spirit in **Set menu 2**, enabling Peter and John to do marvellous things in Jesus name!

For children from other faiths
The concept of faith relates to most religions: a belief in something beyond what is experienced through the five senses. The man's faith in Jesus in this story can be drawn out, as can his submission to the will of God through his encounter with Jesus.

Do you believe in Jesus with all your mind, with all your heart and with all your soul – and does your life act as a witness to your faith?

Here's another challenge: What more can you believe about Jesus today?

Pray together
- Pray for each other to be strengthened in your faith.
- Pray for the day's activities.
- Pray for the children. Ask God to help the children to believe big accurate beliefs about Jesus!

PRACTICAL PREPARATIONS

Talk through the morning's programme, and make sure everyone is aware of his or her responsibilities. Encourage the team to be really welcoming and as interactive with the children as possible. Ensure that all resources are ready for the various activities.

Equipment checklist for Set menu 3
- **Registration** Registration forms, badges, pens, team lists
- **Guest Groups** Bibles, *Rocky's Menus* or *Daily Specials*, pens, Bible discovery notes, 'Believe it or not' questions, wooden cross, paper, pins/Blu-tack
- **Music** The Sardines band all set up or backing tracks
- **Drama** Costumes and props
- **Technology** PA system, laptop, PowerPoints and projection/OHP and acetates, fish of the day and mega game pictures, *Rocky's Plaice* DVD
- **Activities** Equipment for craft and games
- **Maitre D'** Running order, notes, story chest and mat with 'have faith' written on, two T-shirts
- **Refreshments** Drinks and biscuits, or other refreshments
- **Storytelling** Costumes for Peter and John

Serving time

As the children arrive, play lively children's music in the background and display the *Rocky's Plaice* logo on a screen using a data projector or OHP. Register any new children and take them to their groups.

A TABLE FOR YOU
10 minutes

BELIEVE IT OR NOT!

What you need
- Believe it or not! questions from the *Rocky's Plaice* website or DVD

What you do
Go through the questions and ask the children to guess whether they think each question is true or false. When you have finished, ask the children which fact they found the most surprising. If you are having a Cornelius party at the end of the week, tell the children about it today.

RED HOT!
45 minutes

Play the *Rocky's Plaice* song as everyone joins the larger group. Welcome everyone to *Rocky's Plaice* and quickly describe some of the activities in store today. Check to see if the children can remember **Set menu 1**'s key word – 'hope', and **Set menu 2**'s key word – 'be filled'.

RESTAURANT CLEANING CREW
Introduce the cleaning crew, who should lead the children in the same warm up exercises as yesterday. How much of the routine can the children remember?

KEY WORD: HAVE FAITH
STORY CHEST: MAT
Remind the children of the story chest. Bring out the mat and ask the children what it is. Have a creative think together about the mat – what might that tell us about the church? How does it link to the key word written on it: have faith? Tell the children that Christians believe loads of great things about Jesus and they trust him. This means that they have faith in him. Place the mat next to the boomerang and torch.

FISH OF THE DAY
Introduce Mr Tagliatelle, who then tells the children about the fish of the day:

Mr Tagliatelle: Welcome to *Rocky's Plaice* – we have a wonderful selection of beautiful fish for you available on our exclusive menu. Today's fish of the day is called the mudskipper. *(Show a picture.)*

The mudskipper is a fish that can walk on land! They use their fins to 'walk' along the ground and can spend days out of the water. In fact, when they're out of the water they can feed or even fight each other! Well, there probably won't be any fighting today – unless Salt and Vinegar don't behave themselves – but you may see other unexpected things walking today!

MEGA GAME: OUCH THAT HURTS!
Explain the rules to the children and then play the game as described below:

Display a list of six different parts of the body which could be hurt. (There is a list on page 94.) A couple of the team should then go out of sight. Taking it in turns, these two leaders have to shout out as if in pain, for example, 'Ouch, I was riding my skateboard and then…Arrgghhh!' Guest Groups have to guess which part of the body the leader has hurt. The leader then comes out holding that bit of the body, and the groups see if they were right. Make it quick and mad!

SONGS

Ask The Sardines to lead the children in the *Rocky's Plaice* theme song, together with two songs you have already sung at *Rocky's Plaice*.

RED HOT NEWS

Introduce Captain Ketchup and Red Hot News:

CK: Good morning everyone, and welcome to Red Hot News. It's time to do the ketchup dance! *(Everyone does the ketchup dance.)* Thank you! This is Red Hot News – helping you ketch-up with the news! Ooh, it's hot!

Hot News! There is definitely a big celebration here at *Rocky's Plaice* on the last day. Hurrah! I had a very funny dream last night – I had party ring earrings on, with a party ring also stuck on the end of my nose. I actually looked a bit stupid!

Hot News! Salt and Vinegar are determined not to make a mess today! Mr Did-I-see-you-on-the-telly has got some great new names!

Hot News! The Deep Fat Fryer is very excited about the pictures of Scraps!

Hot News! Edna, my pet hamster, has been squashed by a bus! Whoa! *(Pretends to cry.)*

Hot News! The key word for today is 'have faith'. It's all about believing and trusting!

Hot News! Peter is back again! And that's the news this morning!

Maitre D': That is great news CK – we'll see you tomorrow. Big clap for Captain Ketchup! Boys and girls, a big welcome for Peter!

(Adapt the ending of Red Hot News to fit your particular storytelling choice.)

STORYTELLING

Welcome Peter on stage and perform this script. Alternatively, introduce the DVD and show episode 3 to the children. You might be using both; in which case, show the DVD after Peter and John have left the stage.

Maitre D': Hi Peter, it's great to see you again!

Peter: Hi everyone, it's great to see you in *Rocky's Plaice*.

Maitre D': Peter, we've had a boomerang and a torch so far… today we've got a mat! What story goes with a mat?

Peter: Oh, the mat story! It's another great story.

John: Psst – Peter, are you busy?

Peter: John, John, come on in, welcome my old friend! Boys and girls, this is John. John and I were there on the Day of Ascension, when Jesus went up into heaven. And we were there on the day the Holy Spirit came. What was it called children? That's right – the Day of Pentecost.

John: Hi everyone! Are you just about to tell the mat story? That was the day we got in a load of trouble!

Peter: A load of trouble, what do you mean?

John: Before the Day of Pentecost we'd all been a bit scared of being arrested and killed like Jesus, but suddenly when the Holy Spirit came, we were up for anything and telling everyone about Jesus – we were filled with God's power. Do you remember that day when we went to the Temple to tell people about Jesus? It was about three o'clock in the afternoon and there was that lame man – Simeon I think – he was 40 years old and had never walked?

Peter: I know Simeon – Simeon became a very good friend!

John: Well, Peter and I were on our way to the Temple when we saw Simeon at the gate. He was begging for money – he had to do it of course, because he couldn't walk and earn money himself. He was begging and asking for money. Like this. *(John gets down on ground, pretending to take the role of Simeon.)* Then, God the Holy Spirit in us suddenly gave us both a really strong belief that Jesus wanted to heal him! I told him, 'Look at us.' Well Simeon looked at us expecting to get some money, and then… what did you say to him Peter?

Peter: I said, *(Stands over John.)* 'I don't have any silver or gold, but I do have something else I can give you. By the power of Jesus Christ from Nazareth, stand up and walk!'

John: Well, this poor man couldn't believe his ears – get up and walk? In the power of Jesus? *(Peter should help John up and John should act accordingly.)* Well, we helped him up, and as he stood up his feet and legs became strong, and it was only moments before this man, who had never walked before, was walking and jumping and praising God! Well, we caused a commotion that day! All the people who saw him walking recognised him as the man who always sat by the Beautiful Gate begging for money – they were amazed.

Peter: Jesus is wonderful, isn't he? Simeon's life had been turned upside down, like so many other people's!

John: The Jewish leaders didn't like it, but it gave you the opportunity to tell everyone all about Jesus and to encourage them to believe in him. That man was healed because we believed in the power of Jesus and trusted he would heal. Being a Christian is all about believing in Jesus and trusting him – that's called faith! Not just in your head, but living for him every day.

Peter: Many more people became Christians that day… I think we were up to about 5,000 or so. The believing church was growing quickly, with God doing loads of amazing things! God did it!

John: Just fantastic!

Peter: Yep. Three great stories so far: The Day of Ascension (when Jesus went to heaven), The Day of Pentecost (when the Spirit came) and the day when Simeon got healed! God bless, bye!

They leave, chatting excitedly to each other.

MAITRE D'S RECOMMENDATIONS

Thank Peter and John, and then ask the children why the story was the story of the mat. Remind the children of the key word for the day: have faith. What do they think the people who saw this man who couldn't walk being healed might have believed? Get some answers from the groups. Then say that while the man was leaping about on his newly working legs, Peter told the people who were listening about the most important Christian belief. All about Jesus, and how they needed to believe and trust in him: how they had to have faith!

SONGS

After the story, it might be appropriate to sing a song to reinforce the teaching. For example:
- 'Peter and John went to pray' *Junior Praise* (Collins)
- 'Anyone can come to God' *Reach Up!* (SU)

After the songs, announce who the Dish of the Day is later on, and encourage the groups to think of questions to ask the team member. Send everyone to their groups to explore the story of Peter and John some more.

ICE CREAM CRAZY

45 minutes

THE REFRESHMENT ZONE

Serve the refreshments and chat together about the club. What do the children think of the story? Remind the children to think of a question to ask the Dish of the Day. Do the children have any jokes or pictures for the Deep Fat Fryer?

LUKE'S SCROLLS

With older children

Read Acts 3:1,2. Decorate the Beautiful Gate on pages 20 and 21 and wonder why the man had to beg by the entrance to the Temple. Then go on to read Acts 3:3–10 (from page 22 or a Bible), stopping to draw the man in various states of not being able to walk and walking!

Summarise verses 11 to 21, but talk about verses 12 and 16 in particular, as these focus on the fact that the man had faith in Jesus. Look at page 24 and talk to the children carefully about what it means to have faith. Faith can be used sometimes as a jargony word, but it is an important concept when talking about being a Christian.

Look at page 26 together and chat about the different people we have faith in. Have a silly explanation ready (maybe about having faith in your football team and being let down). Explain that it's good to have faith in some people, but not everybody. Talk about why you have faith in Jesus and how you show this in your every day life.

With younger children

Decorate the picture of the Beautiful Gate on the *Daily Special*. As you work, tell the children about why beggars sat next to the Temple (they could not work, begging was their only income, people regularly went to the Temple, so there would be lots of people to ask for money).

Read or retell Acts 3:1–11 to the children. Stop at verses 2, 7 and 8 and ask the children to draw the man at these points (verse 2: lying down; verse 7: being helped up; verse 8: jumping about). Crack the code to find out how the man was made better. Explain that the man believed that Jesus could make him better and trusted him to do so. He had faith! If appropriate, give a few examples of when you visibly put your faith in Jesus.

With all age groups

Adapt these questions to suit your group, sharing your own feelings, opinions and experiences as appropriate:
- How was the man made better?
- How would his life be different now he could walk?
- Who do you know that is sick that needs Jesus to make them better? Pray for them now.
- How can we put our faith in Jesus?
- What do you think of the story of the man who couldn't walk?

CRAFT AND GAMES

Choose a craft activity for today, along with a selection of games that would be suitable for your club. Craft and games activities are on pages 27 to 29. For extra ideas, see *Ultimate Craft* (SU, 978 1 84427 364 5) and *Ultimate Games* (SU, 978 1 84427 365 2).

EXTRA MEATY!
25 minutes

Welcome everyone back together by singing a song you have already sung during the session.

THE SIZZLER
Ask the question, 'Why do Christians believe Jesus died?' and give the Guest Groups a minute to discuss the answer. Then get some feedback.

Show the children a T-shirt that is a total wreck – torn, dirty, marked, creased etc. This T-shirt represents all the bad things in the world and all the bad things we do. Why did Jesus die? So that we can be forgiven. Put the dirty T-shirt in a bag and swap it for a brand new one. Because Jesus took the punishment for all our sin, he can make us clean like this T-shirt – we can be forgiven and start living as friends with him. Tell the children that this offer is open to them. Show the children 1 Peter 3:18 to reinforce the message.

DEEP FAT FRYER
Welcome the Deep Fat Fryer. Ask them to read out some of the jokes from the children and to show some of the pictures of Scraps with his massive breakfast! The Deep Fat Fryer should thank the children, before telling them why Scraps can't join them today – he's had his hair coloured and it turned out to be a real mess! The Deep Fat Fryer should ask the children to draw a picture of Scraps with his terrible multicoloured hair.

LEARN AND REMEMBER VERSE
If you have sung the Learn and remember verse song, then sing it again today. Can any of the children sing it without looking at the words?

Alternatively, gather as many different colours of paper as you have Guest Groups. Write out John 3:16, one word per sheet of paper. Write it out several times more on different colours, until you have enough Learn and remember verses for all the Guest Groups. Hide the sheets of paper all around the room. Explain to the Guest Groups that they have to look for all the words to the Learn and remember verse in their particular colour, bring them back to their group area and arrange the words in the right order.

DISH OF THE DAY
Invite the Dish of the Day to talk to the children about why they have faith in Jesus. Before the session, make sure this is a simple story and one that the children can relate to. Ask the team member one or two of the children's questions too.

THE ADVENTURES OF SALT AND VINEGAR
Introduce the next episode of the drama, the script is on page 36. After some interesting pie combinations yesterday, Salt and Vinegar are asked to make a celebration cake. But how do they make it talk?

EXTRA MEATY FINALE!
Ask the children for some suggestions of things they have learnt today. Finish off Extra meaty! by saying thanks to God for everything you have learnt and pray about the rest of the day. Sing the *Rocky's Plaice* song and send the groups off to the Get your coats time.

GET YOUR COATS
10 minutes

Chat about the highlights of the day and then go on to the prayer activity.

CREATIVE PRAYER

What you need
- A small wooden cross
- Paper and pens
- Drawing pins or Blu-tack

What you do
Set up the wooden cross in the middle of the group. Give the children some small pieces of paper and ask them to draw or write something they'd like to pray for on the sheets. These could be prayers of forgiveness, thanks or asking God for something. When the children have finished, show them how to fix their paper to the cross. Give the children a moment to be quiet and reflect, and then finish the activity with a prayer.

If there is any time left, you could finish Daily Specials or any pages from *Rocky's Menu*. Alternatively, carry on with your Guest Group poster from yesterday's A table for you. As the children leave, remind them of the next session. If you are holding a Cornelius party, encourage parents to come, if you get to the chance to speak to them. Guest Group Leaders should know how each of their children is getting home.

TEAM CLEAR-UP
30 minutes

After the team have cleared up, meet together to debrief. Use the feedback system that works best for you. Have a brief time of prayer where Guest Group Leaders and assistants pray for their groups and other team members pray for their areas of responsibility. Finish by doing any preparation necessary for the next session.

PHOTOCOPIABLE PAGE

ROCKY'S Plaice Set menu 3
Daily special

Today's story is about a man who couldn't walk, who sat next to an entrance to the Temple called the Beautiful Gate.

Can you decorate the Beautiful Gate?

Listen to the story of the man who couldn't walk (it comes from Acts chapter 3 in the Bible).

Draw a picture of the man as he meets Peter and John, and hears about Jesus.

VERSE 2

VERSE 7

VERSE 8

How did Peter say the man was made well? It wasn't Peter, but...

Crack the code to find out!

a	e	i	u

F__th __n J__s__s.

Set menu 4
Dorcas

In the kitchen

SPIRITUAL PREPARATION

Read together
Read Acts 9:36–42.

Talk together
Before sharing the thoughts below, briefly discuss these questions:
- What impact did Dorcas have on the church in Joppa?
- Make a list of all ways the church today can show God's love to people.

Share together
Peter was really struck by the impact of the death of Dorcas. It moved him to pray for her resurrection, a prayer that God graciously answered.

God's people have always been called to love and care for each other and to love the people around them. The description of Dorcas in this passage reads: 'she was always doing good things for people and had given much to the poor.' Sometimes the church can get so busy with meetings and committees that it becomes too busy to tell other people the good news; too busy to do good works and too busy to help the poor.

James wrote: 'Faith that doesn't lead us to do good deeds is all alone and dead' (James 2:17). Dorcas was a great example of a lady who showed her love for Jesus by loving the people around her.

Maybe Dorcas ended up with these words on her tombstone: 'she was always doing good and helping the poor.' Could such a phrase be written about you?

Setting the table

KEY STORY
Dorcas – Acts 9:36–43

KEY THEME
Jesus' followers should be a loving, caring community who reach out in love.

KEY AIMS
- To tell the story of how Dorcas helped the church love the poor.
- To understand the biblical concept of love in action.

For children with no church background
Dorcas coming back to life dominates this story and could lead you into some difficult discussions about God reviving relatives if they are nice and you ask him to. Be prepared for any such questions but don't linger on them. Instead, focus on how Dorcas loved those around her.

For church children
Focus on Dorcas' character with children from a church community. How does loving God affect their lives? It feels good to do nice things for others but challenge children to think about why Dorcas did what she did.

For children from other faiths
That Jesus advocated a life of love is one of the hallmarks of Jesus as being recognised as a significant character in some religious traditions. One may say that love was central to the teachings, life and philosophy of Jesus. This continued through the stories of Paul and is central to the message of the New Testament.

Pray together

- Pray for each other as you show the love of Jesus to all the children today.
- Pray for the day's activities.
- Pray for the children. Ask God to really encourage the children to care for people they know and the poor.

PRACTICAL PREPARATIONS

Talk through the morning's programme, and make sure everyone is aware of his or her responsibilities. Encourage the team to be really welcoming and as interactive with the children as possible. Ensure that all resources are ready for the various activities.

Equipment checklist for Set menu 4

- **Registration** Registration forms, badges, pens, team lists
- **Guest Groups** Bibles, *Rocky's Menus* or *Daily Specials*, Bible discovery notes, pens, clothes shapes, art materials, washing line and pegs, red paper hearts, sticky tape/Blu-tack
- **Music** The Sardines band all set up or backing tracks
- **Drama** Costumes and props
- **Technology** PA system, laptop, PowerPoints and projection/OHP and acetates, fish of the day and mega game pictures, *Rocky's Plaice* DVD
- **Activities** Equipment for craft and games
- **Maitre D'** Running order, notes, story chest and coat with 'love' written on, red paper hearts
- **Refreshments** Drinks and biscuits, or other refreshments
- **Storytelling** Costumes for Peter and Dorcas

Serving time

As the children arrive, play lively children's music in the background and display the *Rocky's Plaice* logo on a screen using a data projector or OHP. Register any new children and take them to their groups.

A TABLE FOR YOU

10 minutes

Welcome the children and remind them to put a joke or picture in the Deep Fat Fryer's chip pan, if they have brought one. Remind them too of the Cornelius party, if you're having one. Then go on to this activity.

WASHING LINE

What you need

- Clothes shapes cut from coloured paper (for templates, go to the *Rocky's Plaice* website or DVD)
- Felt-tip pens or other art materials
- Length of washing line and pegs

What you do

Let the children choose a clothes shape and encourage them to decorate it on one side. Have fun making these clothes and, as you work, chat about those people who provide their clothes for them, maybe parents, grandparents, carers etc. When the children finish (it's not important that they finish now – this could be continued in Get your coats), peg their clothes to the washing line.

RED HOT!

30 minutes

Bring A table for you to a close and draw everyone's attention to the front. Welcome the children to *Rocky's Plaice* and especially welcome any new children for the day. Explain something of what the children can expect today. Check to see if anyone can remember the key words so far: hope, be filled and have faith.

RESTAURANT CLEANING CREW

The cleaning crew leads the club in the daily workout. Introduce a new exercise today, as well as some of the old ones, to challenge the children!

KEY WORD: LOVE
STORY CHEST: COAT

Remind the children of the story chest. Bring out a coat and ask the children who they think may have worn the coat. Have a creative think together about the coat – what might that tell us about the church? How does it link to the key word written on it: love? Tell the children that Christians believe that God loves everyone deeply. God wants his people to love each other and to love the people of the world.

FISH OF THE DAY

Introduce Mr Tagliatelle. He then tells children about the fish of the day:

Mr Tagliatelle: Welcome to *Rocky's Plaice* – we have a wonderful selection of beautiful fish for you available on our exclusive menu. Today's special fish of the day is called the leatherjacket fish. *(Show a picture)*

This fish is found off the shores of Mexico. It has thick leathery skin, a bit like a leather jacket! I like jackets a lot – I have leather ones and rainproof ones, light ones and heavy ones, buttons and zips, hoods and pockets – but none made out of fish! Look out for someone today who was good at making coats, cloaks, tunics and more! Have a beautiful day!

MEGA GAME: 'HEART PAIRS'

Explain the rules to the children and then play the game as described below:

Display the picture from page 95 (there is a colour version on the *Rocky's Plaice* website and DVD) and give out blank grids to the Guest Groups. There are eight pairs of hearts – give the Guest Groups a minute to remember where all these pairs are. At the end of the minute, remove the picture and ask the groups to write on their grid where they think all the pairs are. When everyone is finished, show the picture again and ask the Guest Group Leaders to check how their group did.

SONGS

Sing the *Rocky's Plaice* song with the actions, together with one or two lively songs that have been popular during the club.

RED HOT NEWS

Introduce Captain Ketchup and be ready to join in the ketchup dance!

Captain Ketchup: Good morning everyone, and welcome to Red Hot News. It's time to do the ketchup dance! *(Everyone does the ketchup dance.)* Thank you! This is Red Hot News – helping you ketch-up with the news! Ooh, it's hot!

There's only one day left until the celebration here at *Rocky's Plaice*! Hurrah! A massive thank you to everyone who has brought me party rings – I had party ring sandwiches for lunch yesterday, party rings, chips and peas for tea and party rings on toast for breakfast! Yummee!

Hot News! Salt and Vinegar will be back later – hoping to win some more silver stars!

Hot News! The Deep Fat Fryer thinks your pictures of Scraps are superb! He'll show you some of those later too!

Hot News! Ant and Dec will be hosting *I'm a Gerbil, Get Me Out of Here.*

Hot News! The key word for today is love. *(Sings an appropriate song with the word 'love' in it.)* Wehey!

Hot News! I can hear Peter's back again! And that's the news this morning!

Maitre D': That is great news CK – we'll see you tomorrow. Big clap for Captain Ketchup! Boys and girls, a big welcome for Peter!

(You will need to amend this last section of Red Hot News if you are using the DVD rather than the Peter storytelling.)

STORYTELLING

Welcome Peter on stage and perform this script. Alternatively, introduce the DVD and show episode four to the children. You might be using both; in which case, show the DVD after Peter and Dorcas have left the stage.

Maitre D': Hi Peter, it's great to see you again!

Peter: Hi everyone, it's great to see you again.

Maitre D': Peter, we've had a boomerang, a torch and a mat – now we've got a coat!

Peter: Oh, you'd like me to tell you the old coat story! It's another great story, you know! I've already told you three great stories of how the church started. Hands up if you can tell me who had just gone back into heaven on the Day of Ascension? That's right, it was Jesus. Can someone tell me who came on the Day of Pentecost? That's right, God the Holy Spirit. Then yesterday we heard about Simeon – the day he was healed and able to walk after 40 years. Great stories! The church was growing all the time… loads of new Christians!

Dorcas: It caused a few problems though! Hi there Peter!

Peter: Dorcas, oh Dorcas, it's great to see you! Come, come and take a seat. Boys and girls, this is my friend Dorcas – welcome to *Rocky's Plaice*!

Dorcas: It's lovely to see you Peter; you're looking as young as ever!

Peter: You're so kind to say so – in fact you, Dorcas, are one of the kindest people I know!

Dorcas: Well isn't it what the church is supposed to be, Peter – kind, caring, to look after people and to love them all?

Peter: You're right, and we tried to do that as best we could. I can remember early on, when we had well over 5,000 people in the church, just a few of us tried to care for all 5,000 people. We'd do the washing up, make sure people had food, pray for people, teach people and do about 100 other things at the same time. Doing everything became impossible for just 12 of us! In the end some people were not cared for as well as they should have been.

Dorcas: You did the right thing though Peter, because you and the other leaders listened to God. You chose some loving and caring people, like that lovely man

Stephen, to take care of the poor and needy so that you could spend a bit more time teaching people, praying and leading the church. None of us can do everything! Oh, and Stephen was a lovely man. He made sure that the church really cared for the people in need. People like the widows who had no money. Like the children who had no parents. Like the sick and the hurting. We prayed for people and we cared for people – that's what I think the church should do!

Peter: Well Dorcas, you have always been a champion for the poor. I have to tell you boys and girls, this lovely lady from Joppa should be dead!

Dorcas: *(Pretending to be offended.)* Well, really!

Peter: No, listen! This lady is amazing at making blankets and clothes for the poor. She made the most wonderful coats. I remember the time I was in Joppa and all the Christians were really upset – it was because this lady had died! *(Dorcas gets on floor pretending to be dead.)* When I saw everyone so upset, and all the items Dorcas had made, I went to the place where her body lay and I prayed. I prayed that God would send her back to us so she could continue to show God's love to the poor.

Dorcas jumps up, shouts and leaps about.

Peter: And you can see that God did it! Dorcas, you really loved the poor, didn't you?

Dorcas: Not just me Peter; it's what the Church is called to do. I know you cared, and I encouraged everyone to love the people they know – because Jesus loves them.

Peter: The church is called to hope, to be filled, to have faith and to love. It's been great to see you, Dorcas. *(To children.)* And you too! Bye!

They leave, chatting excitedly to each other.

MAITRE D'S RECOMMENDATIONS
Thank Peter and Dorcas. Ask the children why the object from the story chest is a coat today. State that Dorcas was famous for all the lovely coats and other clothes she used to make for people who couldn't afford them. Remind the children of the key word for the day: love. Ask the children why they think that God wants Christians to love other people. Summarise the answers by saying that God is love – in him there is nothing wrong, nothing bad – he is love! He also wants us to be like him and to show his love to the whole world.

SONGS
After the story, it might be appropriate to sing a song to reinforce the teaching. For example:
- 'Taller than the mountains' *Reach Up!* (SU)

- 'For God so loved the world' *kidsource2* (world wide worship)
- 'It's the little things' *Junior Praise* (Collins)

After the songs, announce who the Dish of the Day is and encourage the Guest Groups to come up with questions to ask that team member. Send everyone to their groups to explore the story of Dorcas more.

ICE CREAM CRAZY
45 minutes

THE REFRESHMENT ZONE
In your Guest Groups, have your refreshments together and chat about the club so far. Remind everyone about questions for the Dish of the Day, and about jokes and pictures of Scraps for the Deep Fat Fryer. Then go on to explore the Bible together.

LUKE'S SCROLLS

With older children
Before the session, find out what the names of all the children in your group mean. (Put 'meaning of names' into an Internet search engine.) Using page 28, help the children discover what their names mean if they don't already know. You could turn it into a matching game. Move on to do the clothes picture game on page 29.

Read Acts 9:36–42 (from page 30 or a Bible) and fill in the blank faces on page 31, thinking together about how the people must have felt. Why were the people sad that Dorcas had died? Talk about how Dorcas had showed God's love to them, by making clothes for them (see verse 39). Explain that widows would be very poor, because at that time, it was usually the men who earned money, and they had no man to provide for them.

Go on to think about how you can show God's love to others, chat about appropriate ideas for a while and encourage the children to write down an idea they like.

The session does not concentrate much on the fact that Dorcas was brought back to life by Peter, but the children may well have questions about it. If they'd like to talk about it, then try to answer any questions they have, while not dwelling too long on the subject.

With younger children
Look at the pictures of clothes on *Daily Special*. Can the children tell what they are? (They are: 1 shoes, 2 shirt, 3 T-shirt, 4 trousers, 5 skirt, 6 sunglasses.) Read the story of Dorcas to the children from Acts 9:36–42, or retell it in your own words. Look together at the

picture and decide which picture is most appropriate. Comment that the Bible said Dorcas was always doing good things, so she might have done those other things too!

Encourage the children to write down the names of some of their friends. When they have finished, say a simple prayer thanking God for them, and ask each child to say the names of some of their friends as part of the prayer. Then go on to think about how you could show God's love to those friends. If the children come up with any ideas they'd like to do, then get them to write or draw it in the space provided. The next time you meet, ask the children if they've been able to do it!

With all age groups
Adapt these questions to suit your group, sharing your own feelings, opinions and experiences as appropriate:

- Why were there so many people interested in Dorcas?
- Why did Dorcas spend so much time making clothes for the poor?
- What can we do to show other people God's love?
- What can we do to show other people God's love?
- What do you think of Dorcas' story?

CRAFT AND GAMES
Choose a craft activity for today, along with a selection of games that would be suitable for your club. Craft and games activities are on pages 27 to 29. For extra ideas, see *Ultimate Craft* (SU, 978 1 84427 364 5) and *Ultimate Games* (SU, 978 1 84427 365 2).

EXTRA MEATY!
25 minutes

Welcome everyone back by singing a song you have already sung during the session.

THE SIZZLER
Ask the question, 'How could you show someone you know how much God loves them?' and give the Guest Groups some time to chat about it. Get some feedback and then go on to help the children think more about love.

Have some small red hearts that you can give out to the children as you talk. Refer to some of the children's answers to the sizzler, then talk about Dorcas again, about the ways she loved people. As you mention each thing she did, give a heart to a different child and explain that, when Dorcas gave anyone a gift of clothing, she was giving them some of the love of

God. After talking about Dorcas, talk about some of the love that people have given to you, eg helped you with preparation for *Rocky's Plaice*, made you a meal, given you some presents. Encourage the children that they can give little bits of God's love to others – God loves his church to love!

DEEP FAT FRYER
Welcome the Deep Fat Fryer, who should read out some of the jokes from the children and show some of the pictures of Scraps with his outrageous hairdo! The Deep Fat Fryer should thank the children, before telling them why Scraps can't join them today – he's gone to see his friend because she has made a ridiculous hat for him to wear! Ask the children to draw a picture of Scraps with his outrageous hat.

LEARN AND REMEMBER VERSE
If you are using the Learn and remember verse song, then sing that again together. Can the children sing it without seeing the words?

Alternatively, write all the words on different clothes shapes made from paper (similar to the ones used in A table for you). Have a washing line going across the room, and peg the 'clothes' to it in the right order. Gradually take the pieces of card down as the children learn the verse.

DISH OF THE DAY
Invite the Dish of the Day to come and tell the children what it means to them to be loved by God, how they have been loved by others and how they try to love other people. Ask a couple of the children's questions too.

THE ADVENTURES OF SALT AND VINEGAR
Introduce the next episode of the drama, the script for which is on pages 39 to 40. Salt and Vinegar come up with some strange ways of making mushy peas!

EXTRA MEATY FINALE!
Ask what the childern have enjoyed at *Rocky's Plaice*. Thank God for some of those things and also that he loves us. Sing the *Rocky's Plaice* song and send the groups to their Get your coats time.

GET YOUR COATS
10 minutes

As you sit with your group for the final time today, chat about the highlights of the day, then go on to the prayer activity.

CREATIVE PRAYER

What you need
- Clothes shapes and washing line from A table for you
- Small red heart-shaped pieces of paper
- Pens
- Blu-tack or sticky tape

What you do
Give the children small red heart-shaped pieces of paper. Ask the children to write down or to draw on their individual heart something they would like to do for someone to show them how much God loves that person. Ask the children to stick their hearts onto one of their clothes shapes from earlier in the session. As they stick on the heart, encourage them to ask God to help them.

Alternatively, you could do this as a whole-club activity, and put four large hearts, labelled 'Families', 'Friends', 'School' and 'Neighbours' around the room. The children should stick their small hearts to the most appropriate heart for them.

Remind the children about the Deep Fat Fryer's chip pan and the times for the next session. If you are having a Cornelius party at the end of *Rocky's Plaice*, remind parents about coming. All Guest Group Leaders should know how each of their children are getting home.

TEAM CLEAR-UP
30 minutes

After the team have cleared up, meet to debrief, using the feedback system that works for you. Identify anything that needs reworking for the next session. Staying all together, end with a prayer time, praying for any children in particular who have shown an interest in becoming friends with Jesus. Go on to mention every child in the club by name. Finish by doing any necessary preparation for tomorrow.

PHOTOCOPIABLE PAGE

Daily special

Look at these pictures, can you tell what clothes they are?

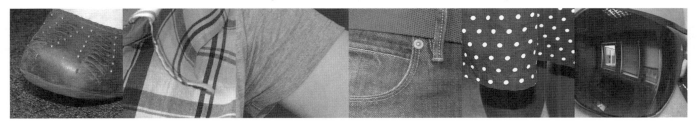

_____   _____   _____   _____   _____   _____

Listen to the story of Dorcas, and decide how she showed people that God loved them.

Circle the right picture.

She made everyone soup.

She made clothes for people.

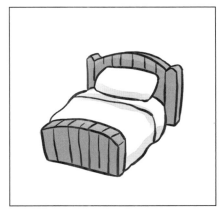

She let everyone stay in her house.

Think of your friends – all your friends.

Write some of their names here and say 'thank you' to God for them.

How can you show people that God loves them? You might not be able to sew very well, but there are other things that you could do!

Write or draw it here.

_____

_____

_____

Set menu 5
Cornelius

Setting the table

KEY STORY
The story of Cornelius – Acts 10:1–29,34,44,45

KEY THEME
Jesus' followers are called to tell the world about Jesus!

KEY AIMS
- To introduce the story of Cornelius
- To understand the biblical concept of sharing the good news!
- To celebrate what Jesus has done by having a party!

For children with no church background
The idea of God's people being separate and not being allowed to mix with other nationalities and religions may seem a strange one to children with little or no church background. The idea that they were not allowed to eat certain meats will also appear unusual. Talk about how God wanted them to be special, and he treated them with care, just like we treat things we want to stay special with care, trying to protect them and keep them safe.

For church children
If children from a church community have heard this story before, help them link it to other stories they already know, maybe about Moses and the Israelites in the desert. It might be useful to use a Bible timeline (such as the one produced by SU, 978 1 84427 362 1) to help children place this story in God's great story of the Bible.

For children from other faiths
This story speaks of inclusion and illustrates that anyone can become a part of God's family. This is a key message for children of other faiths – that no one is outside of God's plan and purpose. All are loved by him.

In the kitchen

SPIRITUAL PREPARATION

Read together
Read Acts 10:1–29,34,44,45

Talk together
Before sharing the thoughts below, briefly discuss these questions:
- Why was this story such a momentous one for the church?
- How many bits of the story could you say 'God did it!'?

Share together
This story reveals a pivotal moment in church history. The church had assumed that the Christian faith was for Jews. The law that Peter had followed throughout his life forbade him from interacting with foreigners and from eating unclean meats, a full list of which can be found in the book of Leviticus.

The story is full of God's initiative, and yet it was in response to Cornelius' prayer and faithful acts of love. God sent a vision to Cornelius. He did the same for Peter, with perfect timing as Cornelius' men had arrived at the door. With the Holy Spirit's prompting Peter went to Caesarea. Then, even as he spoke to those who were listening, the Holy Spirit came powerfully upon them all.

There is no doubt that God had carefully planned this sequence of events – even the sceptical Jewish Christians gave God glory when Peter told them. Acts 11:18 reads: 'When they heard Peter say this, they stopped arguing and started praising God. They said,

"God has now let Gentiles turn to him, and he has given life to them!'"

The vast majority of the Christians in the world today should be thanking God for the wonder of this story, and for how the good news of Jesus has been told to people throughout the world, to people just like us!

Pray together
- Thank God for the wonderful message of Jesus and that his invitation is open to all!
- Pray for the day's activities and for yourselves as a team on this final day.
- Pray for the children. Ask God to touch each individual child today.

PRACTICAL PREPARATIONS
Talk through the morning's programme, and make sure everyone is aware of his or her responsibilities. Encourage the team to make sure they have an individual encouraging word with every child in their group. Ensure that all resources are ready for the various activities. Tell parents that they will be getting a special invite today to the Cornelius party, if you've chosen to hold this event.

Equipment checklist for Set menu 5
- **Registration**: Registration forms, badges, pens, team lists
- **Guest Groups**: Bibles, *Rocky's Menu* or *Daily Specials*, Bible discovery notes, pens, coloured card, art materials, flip-chart paper, marker pen
- **Music**: The Sardines band all set up or backing tracks
- **Drama** Costumes and props
- **Technology** PA system, laptop, PowerPoints and projection/OHP and acetates, Fish of the day and Mega game pictures, *Rocky's Plaice* DVD
- **Activities** Equipment for craft and games
- **Maitre D'** Running order, notes, story chest and sheet with 'tell' written on, four signs : A, B, C, D, sticky dots, fancy stickers
- **Refreshments** Drinks and biscuits, or other refreshments
- **Storytelling** Costumes for Peter and Cornelius

Serving time
Make sure you have started to put up some party decorations. Play some lively party music as the children arrive and display the *Rocky's Plaice* logo. Register any new children and take them to their groups.

A TABLE FOR YOU
10 minutes

Encourage the children to chat with you about the best things from this week at *Rocky's Plaice*. Remind the group to put any jokes or pictures they have brought into the Deep Fat Fryer's chip pan. Remind them too of the Cornelius party, if you're having one.

INVITATIONS

What you need
- Different coloured pieces of card (about A6 size)
- Felt-tip pens or other art materials

What you do
Let the children choose a sheet of card and encourage them to create an invitation for their parent or carer to the Cornelius party, or to the *Rocky's Plaice* Sunday service. Help them with some kind of wording to go on the invitation. As you work chat about what you're going to do at the party/event. Generate some enthusiasm in your group!

RED HOT!
45 minutes

End the Guest Group time by playing the *Rocky's Plaice* song and draw everyone's attention to the front. Welcome the children to *Rocky's Plaice* and especially welcome any new children for the day. Check to see if the children can remember the four key words so far: hope, be filled, have faith and love. Remind the children about the party/event you're going to be having.

RESTAURANT CLEANING CREW
Enjoy the warm-up together. The cleaning crew should do all the exercises you have done during the club so that the children have a big warm up for this final day.

KEY WORD: TELL
STORY CHEST: SHEET
Remind the children of the story chest. Bring out the sheet – what uses can you think of for a sheet? Have a creative think together about the sheet – what might that tell us about the church? How does it link to the key word written on it: tell? Encourage the children that the good news about Jesus is so fantastic, that the whole world needs to be told!

FISH OF THE DAY
Introduce Mr Tagliatelle for his final fish of the day!

Mr Tagliatelle: Welcome to *Rocky's Plaice* – we have a wonderful selection of beautiful fish for you available on our exclusive menu. Today's special fish of the day is a plaice! *(Show a picture.)*

This is *Rocky's Plaice*, so I thought you'd better see a plaice! The three most popular fish in fish and chip shops are cod, haddock and plaice. Plaice is a flat fish that grows to about two foot in length and has a brown spotted body. The great thing about this fish is that it is so beautiful to eat that we want to share it with everyone – indeed that is why I am telling you about it today. I hope you really enjoy your final morning, here in *Rocky's Plaice*!

MEGA GAME: NAME THAT ANIMAL
Explain the rules to the children and then play the game as described below:

Show the children the picture of 12 different animals on page 96 (also available on the *Rocky's Plaice* website and DVD). Give the Guest Groups 30 seconds to memorise the animals, then remove the picture and allow a further 60 seconds for the Guest Groups to write down all the animals they can remember. The Guest Group Leader should be the scribe for their group! Reveal the answers and ask the leaders to see how their Guest Groups did.

SONGS
Choose two lively songs that the children have enjoyed singing through the week, and then sing the *Rocky's Plaice* theme song, together the actions.

RED HOT NEWS
Introduce Captain Ketchup for the final time!

Captain Ketchup: Good morning everyone, and welcome to Red Hot News. It's time to do the ketchup dance! *(Everyone does the ketchup dance.)* Thank you! This is Red Hot News – helping you ketch-up with the news! Ooh, it's hot!

It's the big party day and we'll be partying later! I've got 43 packs of party rings outside and I might just share some with you! I did have 49 packets, but I had one packet for lunch, one for a snack, one for tea, one for supper, one for a midnight feast and one for breakfast. Yummee!

Hot News! Salt and Vinegar are going to be really busy in the kitchen later! I hope they get the last silver stars!

Hot News! Scraps has got his ridiculous hat – some great pictures later!

Hot News! Ant and Dec have been eaten by a crocodile! Whoa! *(Pretends to cry.)*

Hot News! The key word for today is tell – and I've got something really good to tell you! It's party day!

Hot News! I can hear Peter's voice – he's back yet again! And that's the news this morning!

Maitre D': That's great news CK – thank you! Big clap for Captain Ketchup! Boys and girls, a big welcome for Peter!

(Remember to adapt the end of Red Hot News if you're using the *Rocky's Plaice* DVD to retell the story, rather than the Peter script.)

STORYTELLING
Welcome Peter on stage and perform this script. Alternatively, introduce the DVD and show episode 5 to the children. You might be using both; in which case, show the DVD after Peter and Cornelius have left the stage.

Maitre D': Hi Peter, it's great to see you again!

Peter: Hi everyone, I love coming here to *Rocky's Plaice*.

Maitre D': Well, Peter, we've had a boomerang, a torch, a mat and a coat! You'll never guess what the last object is!

Peter: A banana?

Maitre D': Nope!

They go through a few other suggestions, before the Maitre D' pulls out the sheet.

Maitre D': It's a sheet!

Peter: Now the old sheet story is an amazing story. It is one that I've got to tell you!

Cornelius: Praise be to Jesus!

Peter: *(Turning round surprised.)* Cornelius!

Cornelius: *(Embracing.)* Peter!

Peter: Cornelius, take a seat my friend. Boys and girls, this is Cornelius… a friend of mine, a Roman centurion and a friend of God!

Cornelius: Can you remember the early days, Peter? Do you remember all the trouble you had back then?

Peter: Oh yes. There were times when we were arrested and beaten for being Christians. There was the time when Stephen, the chap I was telling the children about yesterday, was killed because he was a Christian. There was the time when Paul (before he became a Christian) used to go around beating all the Christians up. We've had some tough times Cornelius!

Cornelius: We've also had some disagreements with other people in the church too!

Peter: You're right Cornelius. When God puts people together, sometimes people disagree or simply don't get on! It's part of being human – it's how you deal with it that counts. We try to love each other even when we disagree! When I met you it caused me a few problems!

Cornelius: *(All innocence.)* It wasn't my fault! I was at home one day, when I had this vision from God, and God told me that I should send for a man named Peter who was staying in Joppa – near that lovely lady Dorcas. That turned out to be you!

Peter: That's right, and at the same time, I was staying with a chap called Simon, and I was hungry, and I had a vision too. I saw a sheet full of all sorts of animals come down from heaven, and God said to me, 'Get up, Peter, kill and eat.' Well, the things was, I was a good Jew as well as being a Christian. There were some types of meat that I was not allowed to eat, and some I was allowed to eat. But the dream was telling me to eat all the kinds of meat! God was telling me that he loved everyone, not just the Jews.

Cornelius: And just then some of my men had got to Simon's house and were asking for you!

Peter: That's right. Now a good Jew wasn't meant to even talk to someone who wasn't a Jew! But God told me to go with these men, because he had sent them! So I did – and I came with some of my friends to see you. I told you about Jesus and whilst I was still talking God sent the Holy Spirit and filled you all up! It was that day that I discovered that God didn't just want Jews to be Christians; he wanted people like you, Cornelius, and like all these lovely children and adults here, to be Christians – to have faith and be filled!

Cornelius: Not everyone thought it was a good idea to start with though!

Peter: Well Cornelius, you're right. Some of the Jewish Christians found it very hard to believe that people who weren't Jews, like you, could be Christians. But when I told them the story, they were delighted. It was a really important day when you became a Christian – suddenly the good news about Jesus started going to the whole world.

Cornelius: Praise the Lord!

Peter: Praise the Lord!

Cornelius: It's been great to be here, Peter.

Peter: It's been great to see you. *(To children.)* I'll hopefully see you all on Sunday. Goodbye!

They leave chatting excitedly.

MAITRE D'S RECOMMENDATIONS
In this activity the children will end up having a number of dot stickers on their foreheads. Assign four leaders to stand in each corner with A3-sized sheets of paper, marked A, B, C and D. When you ask a question, the children should run to their chosen answer. Choose two of the answer groups to receive a small sticker each. Then go on to the next question.

- **What is your hair colour?**
  A Black, B Brown, C Blond, D Other
- **What is your favourite pet?**
  A Cat, B Dog, C Goldfish, D Other
- **What is your favourite school subject?**
  A Maths, B Art, C Science, D Other
- **How many dots do you have?**
  A No dots, B 1 dot, C 2 dots, D 3 dots

At the end, separate the children into 'dots' and 'no dots' (or 'none and one dot' and 'two or more dots' if there aren't many children with no dots at all). Tell the children that we could say that there is one special group here – the no dot children. Now imagine that in order to stay dot-free, you are not allowed to talk to or even go near any of the dot people.

Before Jesus came, this is how God kept the Jews special. He said to them, 'Don't go anywhere near the people who aren't Jews. Don't marry any people who aren't Jews. Don't eat with anyone who isn't a Jew.'

In today's story, God showed Peter how he wanted things to change. The good news of Jesus might have come to the Jews first, but it was for everyone to share in and so the people who weren't Jews got to hear the good news too! At this point give everyone in the no dot team some special super stickers that they can put on themselves and share with everyone else.

SONGS
After the story, sing some songs to reinforce the teaching further:
- 'Anyone can come to God' *Reach Up!* (SU)
- 'Never, never, never' John Hardwick

After the songs, announce who the final Dish of the Day is and remind the children to put any final pictures or jokes into the Deep Fat Fryer's chip pan. Then send everyone to their Guest Groups to explore the story of Peter and Cornelius more.

ICE CREAM CRAZY
45 minutes

THE REFRESHMENT ZONE
More can be made of the refreshment zone today. It would be great to have a special massive cake that the children can share, or some special celebration party rings! Remind the children about questions for the Dish of the Day, and about jokes and pictures for the Deep Fat Fryer's chip pan. Chat about the day so far

and then go on to explore the Bible story more.

LUKE'S SCROLLS

With older children

Do the picture puzzle on page 33. If you think it would help, you could go on to explain how the Jews had certain foods that they could and couldn't eat. The picture has 11 animals, six of which were considered unclean (pig, camel, crab, owl, badger, snake) and five which were clean (cow, fish, sheep, chicken, deer). Keep your description brief.

The story of Peter and Cornelius is quite a long one, so you may want to summarise sections of the story. Think about how you're going to do this before the session. Break up the story by reading Acts 10:1–12 to start (from page 34 or a Bible), then draw in the space what Peter saw in his vision. Then read verses 13 to 20 and draw what the Holy Spirit said to Peter. Finally, read verses 21 to 30 and draw what Cornelius saw. As you draw each picture, chat about the story so far.

Solve the maze on page 40 and then use verses 34 to 43 to fill in the missing words on page 41. Chat about Peter's message. The children should have picked up what Jesus did throughout the club, but Peter's words here spell it out clearly. What is the children's response to it? Encourage the children to write what they want to say to God in the two speech bubbles on page 42.

With younger children

The story of Peter and Cornelius is a long one, so you'll need to decide before the session how you're going to retell it more simply for children aged 5 to 8. It's probably not appropriate to read the whole passage from the Bible, but mix up reading with retelling. Make sure you include the episodes illustrated on *Daily Special*. When you have finished your retelling, help the children to reorder the pictures on *Daily Special* so that they are in the order of the story.

Recap what Peter says in Acts 10:34–43, outlining what Jesus has done. They will have heard the good news throughout the club, but it will help for you to go over it here. Ask the children what they think of Peter's message to Cornelius and to write or draw it in the speech bubble. Is there anyone else they'd like to tell about Jesus?

With all age groups

Adapt these questions to suit your group, sharing your own views, feelings and stories as appropriate:
- Have you ever been asked to send a message to someone?
- What was the angel's message to Cornelius?
- What was God's message to Peter?

- How did Peter respond to the message he heard and saw?
- Is there anyone you'd like to tell about Jesus?
- What do you think of Cornelius' story?

CRAFT AND GAMES

During the craft and games time, emphasise the party theme by running party-related craft and games, selected from pages 27 to 29. There are more party-related craft and games in *Ultimate Craft* (SU, 978 1 84427 364 5) and *Ultimate Games* (SU, 978 1 84427 365 2).

EXTRA MEATY!
25 minutes

Welcome everyone back together by singing a song you have already sung during today's session.

THE SIZZLER

Ask the question, 'Which one thing about *Rocky's Plaice* would you like to tell someone else?' and give the Guest Groups a minute or so to think about their answers. Get some responses and then recap the five key words – words that everyone in the club might want to use to tell others what has been happening at *Rocky's Plaice*!

Jesus is the Son of God who brings us, and his church, HOPE. He sends us the Holy Spirit so we can BE FILLED. He is the one that Christians HAVE FAITH in. He came to us because God is a God of LOVE and he wants us to love each other. We should TELL everyone about the good news of Jesus.

DEEP FAT FRYER

Welcome the Deep Fat Fryer one last time. Ask the Deep Fat Fryer to read out some of the jokes from the children and to show some of the pictures of Scraps wearing his ridiculous hat!

LEARN AND REMEMBER VERSE

Sing the Learn and remember verse song without showing the words to the children.

Alternatively, repeat the most popular Learn and remember verse activity from earlier in the week. You could also see how many people in each Guest Group can remember the verse!

DISH OF THE DAY

Introduce the Dish of the Day and ask them to say how they have told other people the good news of Jesus, and what the response was. This should be an encouraging story, but should not make the speaker appear super-spiritual or give the children the impression that everyone they tell will get to know

Jesus. This requires a fine balance between inspiration and being realistic. Remember to ask the team member some of the children's questions too.

THE ADVENTURES OF SALT AND VINEGAR

It's time for the final part in The Adventures of Salt and Vinegar. After a busy service in the restaurant, the chefs get a HUGE surprise! The script is on pages 41 to 42.

EXTRA MEATY FINALE!

Finish off the session by saying thank you to God for Jesus, for sending the Holy Spirit and for loving us. Ask God to help us tell others about him. Thank God for all the good times you have had during *Rocky's Plaice*. Sing the *Rocky's Plaice* theme song and send the groups off to Get your coats.

GET YOUR COATS

10 minutes

As you gather in your Guest Groups for the final time, chat about the highlights of the day and the whole club. Then go on to do the prayer activity.

CREATIVE PRAYER

What you need

- Flip-chart paper
- Marker pen

What you do

To finish *Rocky's Plaice*, pray together and tell Jesus what you thought of *Rocky's Plaice*. Ask the children together what they would like to say thank you for, making a careful note on the flip-chart paper. Then ask everyone to stand. The Guest Group Leader or a child can pray the prayer and all the children can be encouraged to give a big shout of 'amen' at the end!

Encourage the children that knowing, following and learning about Jesus doesn't end here! The best way to follow Jesus is with other people's help and as part of a group. If you are holding a Sunday service as part of the club, make sure everyone knows when and where it is. Similarly, make sure the children know all about any Cornelius party you are holding, if this doesn't follow straight after the club. You could hand out information for parents as the children leave.

As the children prepare to leave for the last time, encourage them to take home anything they have made during the club. If you are having a Cornelius party on **Set menu 5**, remind parents of the time it will start and finish and any other details. Each Guest Group Leader should know how each of the children in their group is getting home.

TEAM CLEAR-UP

30 minutes

If you are using a school, or another venue which is not your church building, you may have to have a longer clear-up time today. Remember still to have a debrief time. Ask for some stories of what God has done in children's (and team members') lives during the week. End with a short prayer time, thanking God for all that he has done. Pray too for the children, that you will be able to keep contact and carry on encouraging them. Do any necessary preparation for Sunday's service.

PHOTOCOPIABLE PAGE

ROCKY'S Plaice Set menu 5
Daily special

Peter was about to hear a very strange message. He was going to take Jesus' story to a new group of people! Listen to the story of Peter and Cornelius.

Then put these pictures in the right order. >>>

Peter told Cornelius about the good news of Jesus. At *Rocky's Plaice*, you've heard the good news about Jesus too. What do you think?

Write or draw what you want to say in this speech bubble.

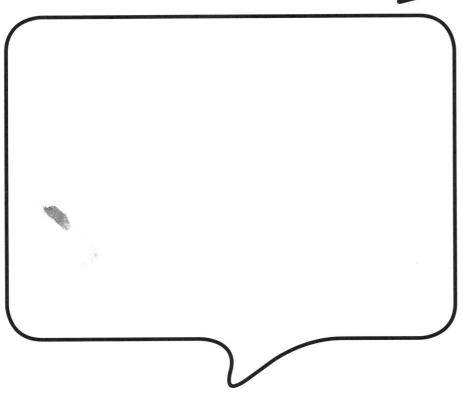

Are there any friends who you'd like to tell about Jesus?

Write their names here!

Special menu **B** Sunday Service 2
Breaking out!

Setting the table

KEY STORY
The prayer meeting and the prison break – Acts 12:1–19

KEY THEME
Jesus calls his people to pray and to expect God to answer their prayers.

KEY POINTS
Jesus loves it when his church prays! A great opportunity to pray for everyone involved in the holiday club and to recap on the key themes covered each day.

Service outline

General welcome
The family service provides the opportunity for some of the craft and Guest Group material from the week to be displayed. If you have gained permission from parents, you might also want to display any photographs taken of the 'action' during the week. Assemble the gallery of work in the entrance as people come in to the church, or in an area where you might serve refreshments. Ensure you have team members at the door to welcome holiday club children and their families to the church, and show them where everything is. This will help people feel at ease as they enter a building they may not be familiar with.

Opening worship and prayer
Sing one or two songs of praise to God. Ensure that these songs are simple and do not contain too many difficult or 'religious' words. Include the *Rocky's Plaice* song. Particularly welcome the children and their families who have come to church for the first time today. Pray at the beginning of the service, inviting God to speak to you during this time.

Explain that you have all been discovering what happened to Peter and the other friends of Jesus after Jesus had died and come back to life again. Chat briefly about Ascension, when Jesus went back to heaven; Pentecost, when God the Holy Spirit came; the time when Peter and John healed a man who couldn't walk; the time when Peter brought Dorcas back to life; and when Peter met Cornelius.

Learn and remember verse
You might like to give the children and the team the challenge of remembering the Learn and remember verse for the week. This could also be sung together.

Holiday club feedback
Invite children and adults who were involved in the holiday club to share a good memory from the week. They might also want to share what they learnt and what the week has meant to them.

The Adventures of Salt and Vinegar
Meet Salt and Vinegar again. Relive the highlights of the week and help them prepare for their first TV show! The script for this is on pages 43 to 44.

Mega game
Choose one of the mega games used during the week, so that those who came to *Rocky's Plaice* have a little advantage!

Songs

Choose one or two of the most popular songs from *Rocky's Plaice*.

Storytelling

Tell the story of the prayer meeting and Peter's miraculous escape from prison. This could be done in a variety of ways:

- Ask the person who played Peter at *Rocky's Plaice* to come and tell the story.
- Prepare a set of pictures and use them to illustrate the story as you read Acts 12:1–19. There are two pictures on the *Rocky's Plaice* website.
- Use the Dramatised Bible to tell the story, or read while actors act out the story. Try to use some of the children who attended *Rocky's Plaice*.

Peter's script

Peter: Hi everyone, welcome to *Rocky's Plaice*. It's been great seeing everyone this week in *Rocky's Plaice*. I'm really glad we've had the opportunity to tell you about the Day of Ascension, the Day of Pentecost, about Simeon being healed, about Dorcas and then about my mate Cornelius!

Rhoda: *(Offstage.)* Peter!

Peter: Who's that?

Rhoda: *(Offstage.)* Peter!

Peter: Rhoda! It's great to see you. Ladies and gentlemen, boys and girls, this is my friend Rhoda.

Rhoda: Did you recognise my voice? *(Giggles.)*

Peter: I recognised your voice, just like you recognised my voice all those years ago!

Rhoda: Oh it was a funny story you know, I still laugh about it every now and then! You were in prison weren't you?

Throughout this next section, Peter and Rhoda act out the story.

Peter: I'd been put in prison by King Herod. This made the Jewish leaders really happy because they didn't like all the great things that were happening to us, including the fact that loads of people were becoming Christians!

Rhoda: You were in prison and I was at home with some of the Christians – we were praying for you and the rest of the church.

Peter: I was locked in the deepest darkest, smelliest, stinkiest prison cell. I'd done a bit of singing and I'd spoken to the other prisoners about Jesus, and then eventually fallen asleep. I thought it was a dream when I was woken by an angel! Then the chains fell off my

wrists, the door opened and the angel led me past all the soldiers who were guarding me – just like that! The angel led me out through the door of the prison and down the road, then suddenly disappeared! It was only then, when I felt the cool of the evening on my face, and I pinched myself (which hurt), did I realise I was really free. So I came as quick as I could to the house where you were praying to let you know that God had heard your prayers. I knocked on the door and called for you to come!

Rhoda: Well, I heard the knock, and when I heard your voice I was so excited that I totally forgot to open the door, and I just went back and told the others that you were there. They didn't think it was you – they thought it might be an angel, but I said no!

Peter: I kept knocking…

Rhoda: And I kept telling them it was you!

Peter: But you didn't let me in!

Rhoda: I did in the end! You told us what happened and then left to find a safe place to stay. Isn't God good – he heard our prayers and rescued you!

Peter: *(Kindly.)* Rhoda, God is always good. It's good to pray and to expect God to answer your prayers.

Rhoda: Yes, I know that now!

Peter: Anyway, time to go – may God bless you all! Bye!

They leave chatting excitedly.

Teaching

Remind the congregation about the story last week: Peter's breakfast with Jesus on the beach. Peter was forgiven by Jesus and called to lead the church. Over this week the children and team have looked at five key stories in the life of the early church along with some key words to help us learn what it means to follow Jesus as part of his people. Ask the children if they can remember from the story chest object, and the key word written on it, what the five stories have been.

- **Day of Ascension:** HOPE (boomerang)
- **Day of Pentecost:** BE FILLED (torch)
- **Healing of the man who couldn't walk:** HAVE FAITH (mat)
- **Story of Dorcas:** LOVE (coat)
- **Story of Cornelius:** TELL (sheet)

In the story today the church prays. Jesus loves his church – he loves them to hope, be filled, have faith, love and tell the good news. A vital part of the relationship that God has with his people is in prayer. God loves to hear prayers and to answer them! Many people would have actually been very surprised to find Peter at our doorway, even after praying for his release. God can, and does hear our prayers. Encourage the congregation to be a praying people. Finish the teaching by praying for the children who came to *Rocky's Plaice*.

Creative prayer

Give each person a sheet of A4 paper and ask the congregation to write anything they'd like to pray for onto the sheet of paper. Be as encouraging as you can, as they may be people who aren't used to praying. Then demonstrate how to make a paper aeroplane out of the paper. When everyone has turned their paper into an aeroplane, together throw your planes around the room. Each person should then pick up someone else's aeroplane and pray that prayer on their behalf out loud and altogether! Repeat the plane throwing and out-loud prayer.

Closing worship

Sing one or two songs to finish, including the *Rocky's Plaice* song, before finishing with a closing blessing.

Refreshments or meal

After the service, provide refreshments for everyone, and make sure team members talk to the families of the children in their groups. If you have time, facilities and space, provide a meal for everyone and play one or two games from *Rocky's Plaice*.

Sixth course Following up *Rocky's Plaice*

Anyone for seconds?

Follow-up ideas

During your holiday club week, you will more than likely make contact with children and families who have little or no regular contact with church. At *Rocky's Plaice* the children will have heard truths from the gospel, built positive relationships with your team and enjoyed being in community. It's a long time to wait until you do it all again next year! The following ideas aim to enable you to continue the important work you have begun and begin to disciple the children on a more regular basis, turning your holiday club ministry into a year-round ministry to children who may be currently outside the reach of your church.

FAMILY MINISTRY

It is vital to remember that children are part of families (however they might look) and that mission to the whole family is an essential part of passing on the stories and love of Jesus.

With a view to reaching the whole family, start inviting them to belong to the community, through events and in developing relationships. Once good relationships have been established, personal faith might be shared. This might take a long time to develop, but long-term commitment to children and families is essential. The ideas here will provide you with some starting points for continuing the work with the children and for connecting with whole families.

Top Tips on Growing faith with families
SU 978 1 84427 249 5 £2.99 is full of helpful advice if you're looking to start a family ministry.

AFTERNOON/EVENING ACTIVITIES

The *Rocky's Plaice* daily outlines provide enough material for one session: morning or afternoon. However, depending on the energy levels of your team and financial resources of your children/families/church, the holiday club lends itself to an optional extended programme, which could involve cookery classes where children learn simple cooking skills (hoping to be better than Salt and Vinegar!), or you could put together a picnic or barbecue. You could run games and/or craft afternoons, using some of the more popular choices in *Rocky's Plaice*, together with options you didn't have time to try out during the club. You could even have some kind of junior Masterchef competition!

Events like these can be used to extend the *Rocky's Plaice* theme over the whole summer holidays, with afternoon or evening events taking place in the weeks following the club.

FAMILY REUNION EVENING

A family reunion event, which could be held in a half-term following *Rocky's Plaice*, allows children to revisit the ideas and themes of the club and to show their families the kinds of thing they were involved in. Try to have most of the *Rocky's Plaice* team available, as this will help children maintain the relationships they had at the club. Here is a suggested programme:

A table for you

As the children arrive, they should go to their Guest Groups to catch up with each other. Play a game where you throw a dice and then talk about a specific topic assigned to the number you throw. Topics could include 'What I remember about *Rocky's Plaice*', 'What I did for the rest of my holidays' or 'What I like best about school'.

Meanwhile parents could either join in with the groups or have a drink in a cafe area, where photographs and pieces of artwork from the week are displayed. Make this environment as warm and welcoming as possible and ensure that a number of team members are available to talk to parents and welcome them as they arrive.

Red hot!
Sing the *Rocky's Plaice* song and play one of the mega games from the club. Explain the stories and themes of each day in the club. You could retell the most popular story from the week too.

Ice cream crazy
Play some of the most popular games from *Rocky's Plaice*; you could even encourage the parents to take part!

Song and prayer
Choose a favourite song from the week to sing together, and then end with a prayer. Thank the parents for sending their children to the club and provide information about other up-and-coming events to be held at church.

Food
Share a simple meal together.

MIDWEEK CLUBS
An ideal way to maintain contact with children is to hold a midweek club at your church or local primary school. Scripture Union publishes eye level resources, aimed at midweek clubs for primary age children, especially those with no church background. *Take Away* is an eye level club specifically designed to follow up *Rocky's Plaice*. This will allow you to carry on the food theme and will explore stories of one of the other heroes of the early church, Paul.

So Why God?, another eye level club, is suitable if you have children who are interested in knowing more about being a Christian. It takes questions children ask about following Jesus and helps them to come up with an answer. It also leads children in a sensitive way through the process of becoming a Christian. (See the inside front cover for details of *Take Away* and *So Why God?*)

EXTENDED SCHOOLS INITIATIVE
All schools are required to offer care for children before and after school as part of the Extended Schools Initiative. A weekly *Rocky's Plaice* club could become a fantastic follow up to the holiday club, engaging with the children where they are already at – in school. In negotiation with the head teacher and key members of staff, the club would be able to provide creative art workshops for children, including the telling of a Bible story and some opportunity for discussion. This will work best in small groups of no more than 12 children.

ROCKY'S PLAICE DAYS
Day events held throughout the year are good to maintain contact with holiday club children. These are effective when they coincide with a special time of the year: harvest, alternative Halloween, Christmas, new year, Valentine's Day, Easter. Here is a suggested programme:

- **Registration** and **Guest Group** games
- **Red hot!** (with story, teaching, songs, games etc)
- **Games**
- **Break**
- **Small-group Bible exploration**
- **Lunch**
- **Craft**
- **Break**
- **Extra meaty!** (songs, learn and remember verse, recap on story, Dish of the Day)
- **Guest Group** time for interactive prayer and response

You can also adapt *Take Away* for use as various day programmes throughout the year. See the end of *Take Away* for more details.

FAMILY DAYS
The programme above need not be limited to children. There is something spiritual about families sharing and learning together. Ability is not necessary, and the children will enjoy helping other adults in activities with which they are comfortable. Therefore, one option is to hold a *Rocky's Plaice* day where you invite the family members of the children who attended the holiday club (parents, siblings, grandparents, aunts/uncles, godparents – all are welcome)

X:SITE
X:site is a children's event for 7- to 11-year-olds. Each event takes place every two months in towns, cities or whole areas and combines silly games, live music, videos, creative prayer, craft, drama, Bible stories and lots more so that everyone can learn about Jesus and have fun at the same time!

X:site is a great way to encourage children in your church by bringing them together with other children in their community – they will have such a good time that they will want to invite their friends to come too. X:site is organised in each area by a partnership of local churches; Scripture Union is really keen to see more X:site events happening around the country. With your help there could be one nearer you.

Check out our website and if you want to get involved get in touch with us. We would really love to hear from you!

Mega Game 1

Mega Game 2

Mega Game 3

Arm   Head   Leg

Hand   Knee   Back

Colour versions of these pictures are on the Rocky's Plaice website

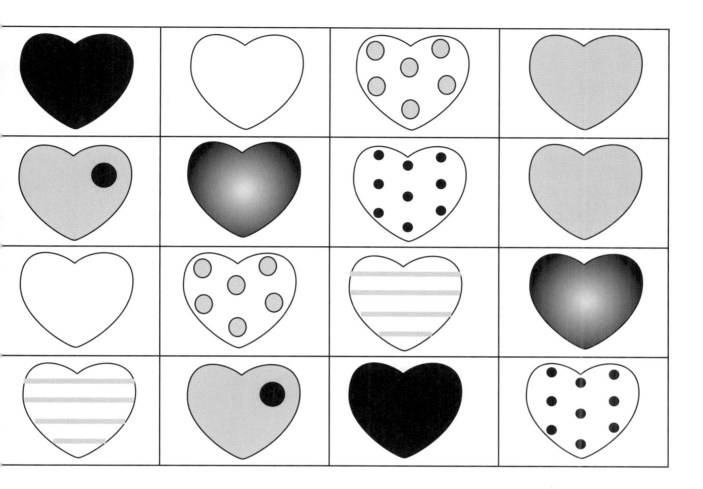

£5 off!

Buy £60 worth of extra
Rocky's Plaice resources and get £5 off!

Complete your name and address, tick the right boxes and cut out the voucher. Then:

- Take it to your local Christian bookshop.
- Send it to:
  Scripture Union Mail Order,
  PO Box 5148,
  Milton Keynes MLO,
  MK2 2YX
  with your order and payment.
- Visit our online shop at
  www.scriptureunion.org.uk and place your order online, where the £5 discount will be applied.

TITLE

NAME

ADDRESS

POSTCODE

EMAIL

We would like to keep in touch with you by placing you on our mailing list. Would you prefer to be contacted by:

☐ post
☐ email
☐ if you prefer not to be contacted, then please tick this box

Scripture Union does not sell or lease its lists.

Mega Game 5

This voucher cannot be exchanged for cash or any other merchandise, and cannot be used with any other offer. This offer includes the *Rocky's Plaice* resource book, *Rocky's Plaice* DVD and *Rocky's Menu* (singles and packs). It does not include CPO merchandise. Only orders of £60 and above qualify for this offer.

To the retailer: Please accept this voucher as a discount payment.

Credit due: £5.00 less normal trade discount.

This voucher must be returned to:
STL Customer Services, PO Box 300, Carlisle, Cumbria, CA3 0QS by 4 September 2010.

NAME OF SHOP

STL ACCOUNT NO

VALUE OF PURCHASE

Cash value 0.0001p

VORP10

Ultimate series

Do you work with children or young people? Need that extra bit of inspiration to help your group explore the Bible? Want that extra idea to complete your session?

Then the Ultimate series is for you! Each Ultimate book is packed full of ideas that have been used successfully by others and are more than likely to work for you! All at £9.99 (except Ultimate Craft, £12.99).

Ultimate Craft 978 1 84427 364 5
Ultimate Creative Prayer 978 1 84427 367 6
Ultimate Games 978 1 84427 365 2
Ultimate Quizzes 978 1 84427 366 9
Ultimate Visual Aids CDROM 978 1 84427 355 3

Order from SU Mail Order
T 0845 07 06 006 F 01908 856 020
www.scriptureunion.org.uk/shop